15

828829

Common dog whelks (*Nucella lapillus*) showing colour variation.
Photo: Douglas P. Wilson, FRPS.

COLLECTING
SEA SHELLS

—

F. D. OMMANNEY

WITH DRAWINGS BY
IVOR KNIGHTON

ARCO PUBLICATIONS

FIRST PUBLISHED 1968 BY ARCO PUBLICATIONS
3 UPPER JAMES STREET GOLDEN SQUARE LONDON WI
COPYRIGHT © F. D. OMMANNEY 1968
PRINTED IN GREAT BRITAIN BY
EBENEZER BAYLIS AND SON LIMITED
THE TRINITY PRESS
WORCESTER AND LONDON

SBN: 209.62560.0

CONTENTS

PLATES

FIGURES IN THE TEXT

COLLECTING SEA SHELLS

1

MOLLUSCS

THE WORD 'shell', like the words 'scale' and 'scallop', comes from the root *skal*, which was common to words indicating 'a hard covering' in the language of the earliest Gothic invaders of northern Europe. In Danish 'shell' is still *skal* but in Scandinavian languages 'sk' and 'sh' are interchangeable so that the Anglo-Saxon invaders of Britain brought 'sh' to these islands as 'shell' but 'sk' as 'scale'. Along the northern coast of Europe, in the Lowlands, the word became *schelpe*, from which the French, who have a distaste for consonants unseparated by vowels, derived *escalope* and we from them in turn derived 'scallop'.

A shell, as we know, may be any kind of hard covering, even that of a projectile, but the vast majority of what we nowadays call 'shells' are the calcareous houses or tests, secreted about themselves for their own protection, of the soft-bodied animals without internal skeletons which belong to the great phylum Mollusca, one of the major groups into which invertebrate animals are classified. Zoologists have long believed that this great group has affinities with that other major group, the Annelida, or segmented worms, of which our common earth worm is a primary example. It seemed probable that the molluscs were descended from a worm-like ancestor although this may seem improbable at first glance. The worms are built on an essentially simple plan while the molluscs are apparently extremely complicated. The body of a worm is a straight tube with another tube, the alimentary canal, inside it. The latter has an opening at the front end, the mouth, for the intake of food, and another at the hinder end, the anus, through which waste matter passes out. But the outer tube, together with many of the structures and organs it contains, the excretory organs, nerve ganglia, muscles and the external appendages as well, is built on a repetitive plan, made up of a succession of almost identical segments.

This supposition, that the molluscs are descended from a segmented worm-like ancestor, received remarkable confirmation in 1952 when the Danish oceanographical research vessel *Galathea* dredged up what looked like some small limpets from a depth of nineteen hundred fathoms in the western Pacific Ocean. On examination these turned out to be living representatives of a class of molluscs only known hitherto as very ancient fossils believed to have become extinct in mid-Devonian times 300 million years ago (see p. 155). Here among molluscs was a case similar to that of the Coelacanth among fish, but even more extraordinary.

The living specimens, and others discovered since then by the U.S. research vessel *Nima*, have now established a new class among living Mollusca, the Monoplacophora (literally, one-shield-bearers). They plainly show in their anatomy the primitive segmented arrangement inherited from a worm-like ancestor. Traces of only eight segments can be seen. The body is bilaterally symmetrical and the alimentary canal is a straight tube with the mouth in front and the anus behind. The breathing organs are five pairs of gills, each a series of membranous platelets attached to an axis, one member of each pair on each side of the body. The muscles, excretory organs, nervous system and other organs all show a segmented arrangement which leads zoologists to believe now that the molluscs, worms (Annelida) and the great group of the Arthropoda (crustaceans, insects, spiders, centipedes, etc.) have all descended from a common soft-bodied ancestor resembling a flatworm (Platyhelminthes) having a short body and a small number of segments.

In the simplest molluscs with which we are ordinarily familiar, and the most primitive until the discovery of the Monoplacophora, the coat-of-mail shells or chitons (Fig. 1a, Pl. 1), traces of the ancestral segmental arrangement can also be seen, but it has been overlaid by molluscan adaptations to a life spent crawling about on rocks. The body is bilaterally symmetrical with a straight alimentary canal. The gills are feathery branching structures arranged along each side of the body under the shell. Although

they seem at first glance to be arranged in pairs they are in fact
derived by multiplication from a single pair. But the animal has
an oval shell like a shield on its back (hence the name *Chiton*, a
shield) divided segmentally into eight plates. The underside of

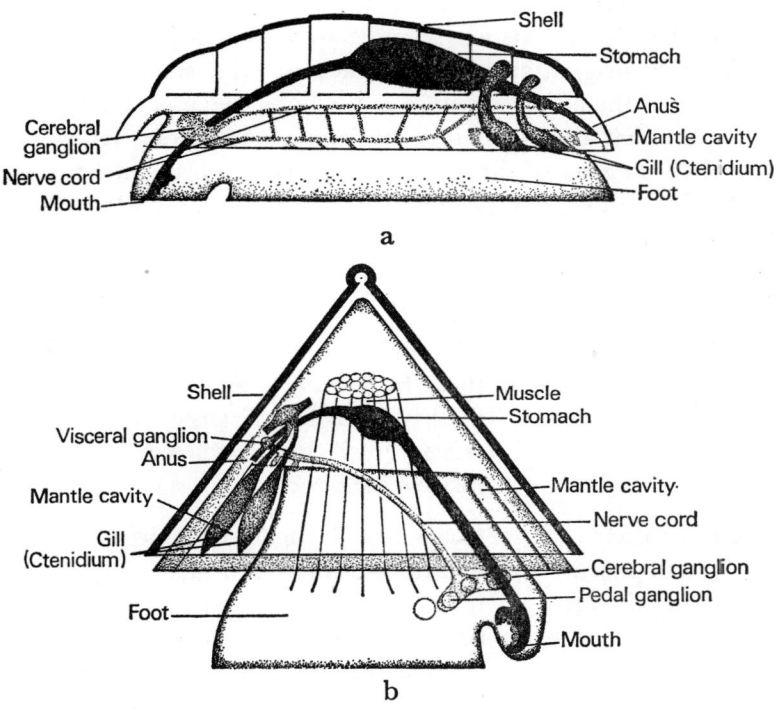

Fig. 1

A. Diagram of a generalized Coat-of-Mail shell, *Chiton*
B. Diagram of a generalized mollusc

the body is thickened and reinforced by muscles so as to form a
flexible contractile foot. With its jointed dorsal shield and flexible
foot the animal can bend itself to fit any surface on which it is
resting. It can, in fact, almost curl itself into a ball like a wood
louse.

All the other molluscs have abandoned the primitive segmental
plan and it is not now discernible in any of them. There are six

main classes of Mollusca in each of which certain common features (Fig. 1b) can be seen although in individual cases these may be secondarily absent, the animal having for one reason or another dispensed with them. Thus, all molluscs have the underside of the body thickened to form a muscular contractile foot, which may be modified in various ways, and they have a fold of skin called the 'mantle' originating along the back on either side of the middle line and, in the adult, enveloping the body like a cloak. It is this which secretes the shell, usually from glands along its margin. The shell consists of three layers, an outer, horny, fibrous one, called the 'periostracum', which oftens wears off, a middle crystalline one, made of carbonate of lime, and an inner pearly one called the 'nacreous layer'.

These six classes of Mollusca are:

1. Monoplacophora: The only living specimens known are those from great oceanic depths dredged up by the research vessels *Galathea* and *Nima*. Fossil specimens from Cambrian to Devonian rocks.

2. Loricata: (Placophora) (Amphineura) Coat-of-mail shells, or chitons, already mentioned. They are bilaterally symmetrical and show the remains of segmentation, oval in shape and flattened, with eight plates, or scutes, on the back.

3. Gastropoda: Limpets, snails, whelks, winkles and other coiled shells, sea hares, sea slugs and the drifting, planktonic sea butterflies.

4. Scaphopoda: Tusk shells. Tube-like, living offshore in sand or mud.

5. Lamellibranchia: Bivalves. Mussels, oysters, cockles, scallops, clams, etc.

6. Cephalopoda: Octopus, squids, cuttles, the argonaut and the pearly nautilus. Only the pearly nautilus among living cephalopods has a shell in the true sense. Many fossil forms which had shells.

The class Gastropoda (3 above) is again divided into three subclasses, the Prosobranchia (limpets, winkles, whelks and other marine coiled shells), Opisthobranchia (sea hares, sea slugs, sea butterflies) and Pulmonata (land and pond snails).

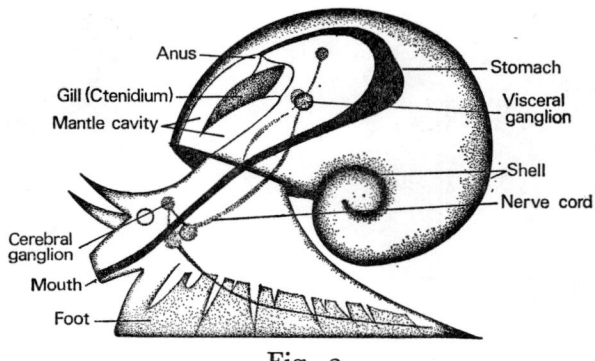

Fig. 2

Diagram of a generalized Prosobranch Gastropod

In the Prosobranchs the body has undergone an extraordinary twisting or torsion through 180° so as to bring the anus and the posterior openings of the excretory organs from their normal position at the hinder end of the body to a new position above the back of the head (Fig. 2). Organs originally on the right side, such as the right-hand member of the pair of comb-like gills, have been carried round to the left side in the twisting process while the originally left-hand organ has disappeared. The main nerve cord, originally a simple loop, has become a figure of eight. In the young of some aquatic snails this twisting process can actually be watched taking place but it is not to be confused with the spiral coiling of the shell which is superimposed upon the body later in life as growth takes place. The animal secretes its shell from the margin of the mantle around the aperture, growing faster on one side than on the other so as to form a spiral. The spiral usually turns clockwise so that the aperture appears on the right hand side when facing the observer (dextral shells). There are some shells, however, such as the American lightning whelk (*Busycon contrarium*), which habitually coil anti-clockwise so that the aperture appears on the left (sinistral shells). All individuals of the same species are commonly either dextral or sinistral but freaks occasionally occur which coil the opposite way to their fellows so that the aperture appears on the wrong side and these

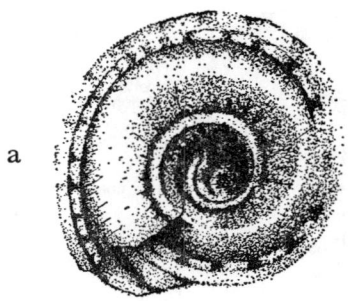

a

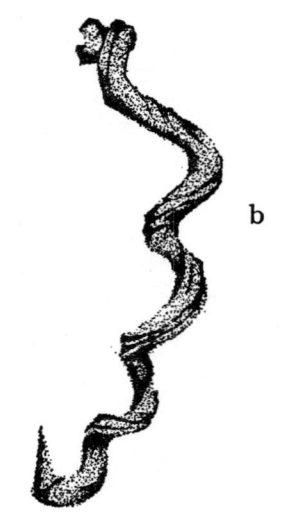

b

Fig. 3: Coiled Gastropods

A. The Staircase shell: *Architectonia perspectiva*, from below, showing the 'umbilicus'.
B. The Corkscrew or Worm shell, Fam. Vermetidae.

rare specimens are very valuable. The snail-like gastropods thus really live in a coiled tube but it is not always very tightly coiled. In those which are not tightly coiled a conical hole can be seen within the whorls when the spiral is turned upside down. This is known as the 'umbilicus' and is visible to a greater or lesser extent in all snail-like shells but in some tropical ones, such as the staircase shells (Architectonidae—Fig. 3a) it forms a deep conical recess into which you can put your finger. That the snail-like molluscs really do inhabit a tube is demonstrated by the tropical corkscrew shells (Vermetidae—Fig. 3b) which begin life growing in a spiral like a snail but later become unwound and continue in a very loose spiral like the stem of a convolvulus plant. In tightly coiled shells the spiral line between the coils is known as the 'suture'.

The limpets at first sight do not seem to be coiled but they are so in youth and only later acquire their conical shape like a Chinese hat.

Most aquatic snails have a horny or sometimes calcareous plate on the back of the foot when extended. This is the door or 'operculum' (literally, 'little lid') by means of which the animal automatically closes its shell when it withdraws. In size and shape the plug exactly fits the opening. The operculum should always be collected with the shell which is not really complete without it. The tropical turbine shells (Turbinidae) have thick limy opercula, convex on one side and flat on the other with green markings. When polished they look like agate and are known as 'cats' eyes'. They are sold in large numbers as ornaments in tropical ports and often may be found lying loose on coral beaches.

In the subclass Opisthobranchia among the Gastropoda the body has become secondarily untwisted. The shell is more or less enveloped in the cloak of the mantle and in most opistho-branchs the shell has become very soft and greatly reduced. It is usually invisible from the outside. In the sea hare (*Aplysia*—Fig. 4) it is a flat, thin, horny disc, completely overgrown by the mantle, and in the sea slugs (Nudibranchia) it has disappeared altogether. In these gastropods the gills have also disappeared and are replaced by frills of the outer skin which often have a tree-like shape or resemble the inflorescence of a flower. Many of the sea slugs are brilliantly coloured and, gliding fully extended among the seaweeds, are among the most beautiful creatures of the seashore. Except for the bubble shells (Bullidae) none of the opisthobranch gastropods have shells which are likely to appear in collections but the subclass includes the great suborder of the sea butterflies (Pteropoda) which drift in the open sea among the plankton. They keep themselves afloat by means of wing-like expansions of the foot which they can flap to and fro. Some are naked but some have delicate paper-like shells, coiled, winged or triangular, and most of them are of small size. They sometimes form vast shoals among the plankton and make up part of the diet of plankton-feeding whales and fishes.

In the subclass Pulmonata the comb-like gills have been replaced for the purpose of breathing air by the development of a lung in the cavity between the mantle and the body (mantle cavity). These are the land and pond snails all of which breathe air to a greater or lesser extent. It is not intended to deal with these in this book.

The gastropods as a class have two methods of breeding. They may either broadcast their eggs and sperm into the sea, as does

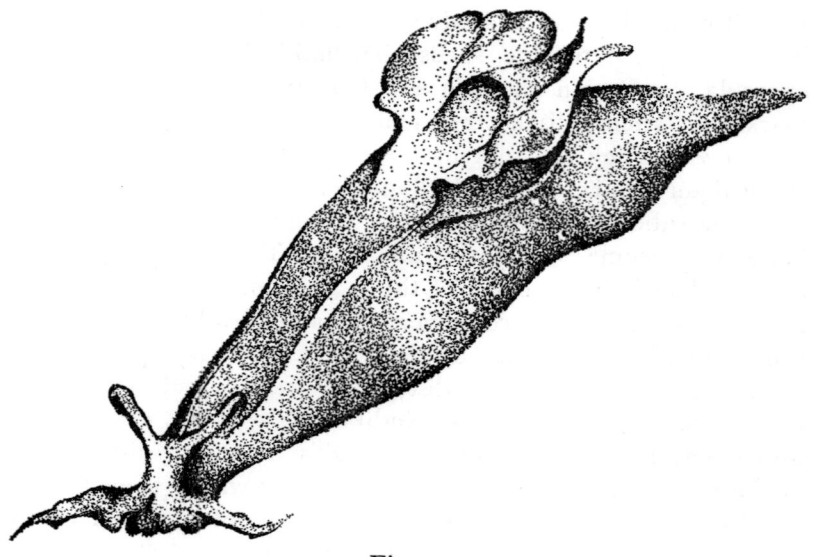

Fig. 4

Opisthobranch Gastropod: the Sea Hare, *Aplysia punctata*, nat. size

the limpet, so that the sperm fertilizes the eggs in the water, or they may produce fertilized eggs from inside the body. In the latter case copulation takes place and the eggs are deposited in clumps or capsules among the rocks and stones. The empty egg cases of the whelk or buckie (*Buccinum*), resembling large dried sponges, are common enough on our beaches washed up along the high tide mark. In prosobranch gastropods the sexes are separate, each individual animal being either male or female, though some, such as the slipper limpet (*Crepidula*), change sex during their lives, being first male and later changing to female. Opisthobranchs and pulmonates are, like the garden snail, hermaphrodite and each individual animal may take either the male or female role.

Some gastropods are herbivorous and some carnivorous. They all feed by means of a rasping organ in the mouth called the 'radula'. It is a long ribbon armed with thousands of minute horny teeth arranged in rows. These teeth grow continually,

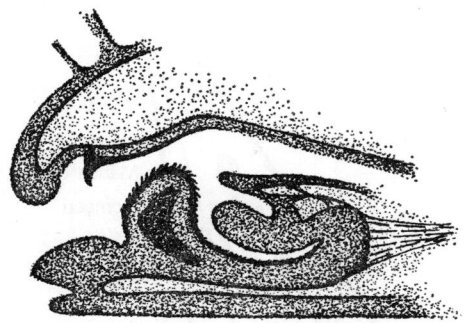

Fig. 5

Diagrammatic longitudinal section of the radula of the Garden Snail, *Helix pomatia*

new ones behind moving forward to take the place of those which wear out. Situated within a pocket inside the mouth cavity the radula is obtruded when the animal is eating and, moving backwards and forwards like a file, rasps off pieces of plant or animal tissue and conveys them to the mouth. The shape and pattern of the radula teeth (Fig.5), as shown by the microscope (for they are minute in size), are very variable and are as specialized, that is, peculiar to each species, as are the form and pattern of the shell. In vegetarian snails the bands of teeth are broad, but in carnivorous ones they are narrow and the teeth prominent so that the radula is more like a drill than a file. It can, and often does, drill holes in the shells of other molluscs. Some of the big tropical cone shells (Conidae) have radula teeth charged with poison from a gland in the mouth. These can be ejected like harpoons so as to inflict quite painful wounds.

Class 4—Scaphopoda (Tusk shells). These are small, delicate, cylindrical shells shaped like a slightly curved elephant's tusk. The shell is a tube open at both ends with the hinder opening smaller than the front one from which the head and foot protrude. Tusk shells live buried head downward in sand or mud in fairly deep water. They may be really looked upon as intermediate in position between the gastropods and the next great class, the

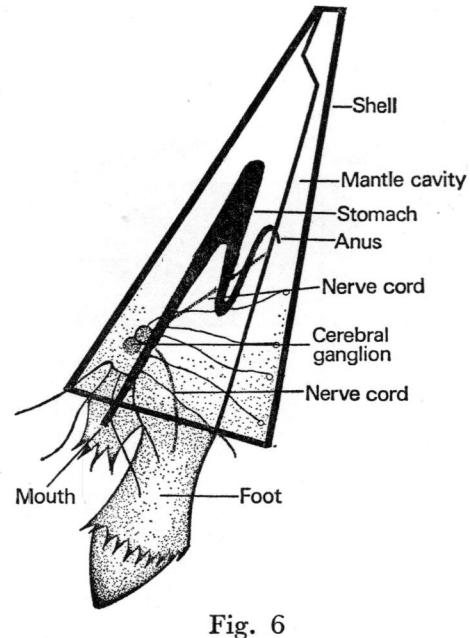

Fig. 6

Diagram of a generalized Scaphopod or Tusk shell

Lamellibranchia or bivalves. No torsion has taken place in the tusk shell body but it is immensely elongated (Figs. 6, 29c) so as to conform with the tube in which it lives, and the lower edges of the mantle have fused, converting the cloak into a tube. The small foot, brought forward to the front or lower opening of the shell, is used for digging and the mouth is surrounded by a ring of fine sensory tentacles, called 'captacula'.

Class 5—Lamellibranchia (Bivalves) (Fig. 7). In this great class of molluscs the mantle is a kind of divided skirt hanging down free as two flaps or curtains one on either side of the body. Each flap secretes a separate shell and the two shells or 'valves' are hinged along the middle line of the back by means of a fibrous ligament and by articulating teeth on the inner faces of the valves. Two strong 'adductor' muscles keep the shell closed, a large one behind and a smaller one in front. These can be plainly seen in

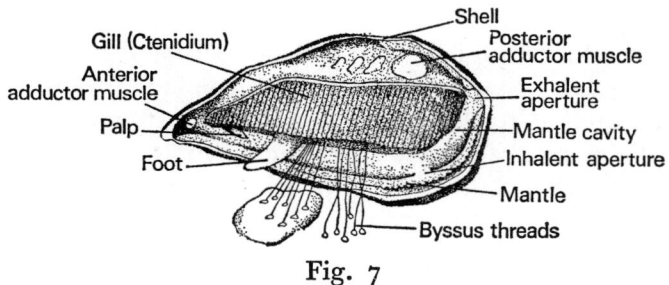

Fig. 7

Diagram of a typical bivalve or Lamellibranch :
the Common Mussel, *Mytilus edulis*

the common mussel, but in many bivalves the front adductor muscle is reduced and in others, such as the oyster and the scallop, the posterior one has become much enlarged and has taken up a central position within the shell. The adductor muscles keep the shell closed by their contraction. When they relax the elasticity of the fibrous hinge between the valves causes them to spring open. The foot has assumed something of the shape of a ploughshare and is used for ploughing through the sand or mud, but it is more or less reduced in those bivalves, such as the oyster and the mussel, which live on rocks or fixed to a firm base. Many of those which live all their adult lives fixed to stones or rocks have a gland beneath the foot which secretes a sticky liquid. The liquid runs down to the tip of the shell, or to that part of it which is applied to the rock, and there hardens into a fibrous attachment, the hairy beard or 'byssus' of the mussel which is so familiar. The byssus is immensely strong as anybody knows who has tried pulling mussels off their rocks. The mussel can inch its way about the rocks by levering itself with its foot so as to snap one lot of byssus threads, secreting another lot on to another part of the rock. Progress by this method is slow but sure.

While the gastropods have a head with well-developed sense organs, tentacles, eyes and so on, the lamellibranchs, being sedentary or at least very slow-moving creatures, and in many cases living quite buried in sand or mud, have dispensed with the head and its associated sense organs. The mouth opens straight into the mantle cavity and usually has two fleshy lobes, the palps, on either side of it which help to select and sort the food.

The lamellibranchs have developed a method of feeding quite different from that of the gastropods, but extremely efficient. Inside the mantle cavity the gills hang down as two or four curtains on each side of the body of the animal forming, as it were, a split petticoat within the covering of the split skirt of the mantle. The gill curtains are made of what might be imagined to be very loosely woven material, built up of long vertical bars separated by microscopically narrow slits forming a grill. The bars are everywhere beset with myriads of minute cilia (protoplasmic filaments) which beat incessantly and automatically so as to cause a current of sea water to flow ceaselessly throughout the life of the animal. The margins of the two skirts of the mantle itself are apposed to one another within the valves except for two openings at the hinder end of the shell. These two openings are called siphons. The sea water current set up by the cilia on the gill bars flows into the mantle cavity through the lower of these two openings in the mantle edge, called the 'inhalent siphon', and, having passed over the gills, flows out through the upper opening, called the 'exhalent siphon'.

No sea water anywhere in the natural state is quite barren of a population of minute microscopic drifting life, both plant and animal. This is called 'plankton' (Greek: something which is caused to wander) and consists of a mixture of many different kinds of plants and animals—diatoms, infusoria, tiny larvae, eggs, minute crustacea and so on. There is also a multitude of decaying animal and plant remains. In our cool northern waters rich clouds of tiny drifting life proliferate in the spring and summer, especially along the shores where vast quantities of microscopic larvae are shed into the sea every spring. These tiny creatures, and much decayed organic matter too, are drawn into the inhalent siphon of lamellibranchs with the water current set up by the cilia on the gills. As the water passes through and over the grill formed by the curtains of the gills the minute life which it carries and the organic matter become entangled by threads of sticky mucus, a sort of saliva, secreted by glands on the gill bars. The cilia on the gill bars are set so that they propel the mucus, and the organic matter it has caught up with it, towards the edges of the gill petticoat and then forward along to the mouth. Here the fleshy palps select the particles. Those that are too large are rejected and pass out of the mantle cavity with the current through the upper or exhalent siphon (Fig. 7). Thus the bivalve mollusc feeds continuously and automatically as long as it is submerged. Out of water the bivalve keeps its valves tightly closed but directly the sea covers it the valves open and gape apart and the animal automatically starts to feed, drawing in a current by one siphon and pushing it out by the other. It follows from this that a bivalve kept in absolutely pure sea water would soon starve to death. But you may wonder how many bivalves manage to feed by this method when living all their lives buried in sand and mud. This problem they solve quite simply by developing a tube like the 'snorkel' of a German submarine. The mantle edges around the inhalent and exhalent siphons are drawn out to form a pair of tubes which reach up from the animal where it lies buried to the surface of the sandy or muddy bottom. In some cases the inhalent and exhalent tubes are joined together, as in the clam (*Mya*—Fig. 25a), and in others, such as the small tellins (*Tellina* —Fig. 22b) and furrow shells (*Scrobicularia*—Fig. 26a), they are quite separate. In some, such as the cockles (Cardiidae), they are quite short (Fig. 19), while in others, such as the tellin (Fig. 22b), they are very long, like hose pipes, several times the length of the shell.

Bivalves that feed on the plankton suspended in the water are known as 'suspension feeders', of which the mussel and the oyster are typical examples. But many of the bivalves that live in sand or mud, such as the tellin, feed more on the fine deposit of dead plant and animal remains on the sea bottom than on living matter suspended in the water. In calm shallow waters, in estuaries and still, sheltered bays, a rain of fine organic refuse settles continually upon the bottom. The buried bivalves suck in this fine detritus layer by means of their inhalent snorkels which in many cases are very long and can be moved about over the sea bottom like the tube of a vacuum cleaner. Molluscs that feed like this are known as 'deposit feeders' to distinguish them from suspension feeders that live on plankton suspended in the water current. There are a few gastropods, such as the pelican's foot snail (*Aporrhais pes-pelicani*) and the tower shell snails (Turritellidae) of our waters that are also deposit feeders (see pp. 110–111).

The lamellibranchs have no rasping radula in their mouths and are all, with a few specialized exceptions, such as wood borers, either suspension or deposit feeders.

The sexes are separate in lamellibranchs but some of them, like some gastropods, change their sex during their lives. The native oyster, for instance, may change its sex several times in a season, being alternately male and then female. The eggs or sperm are shed into the mantle cavity and the individuals are crowded so close together in a colony of bivalves that the sperm is inevitably drawn into the inhalent siphons of neighbouring females. In some cases the eggs go through the early embryonic stages within the mantle cavity of the mother shell and are then set free as larvae into the water. The temperature is the governing factor which triggers off the reproductive process in the spring, in molluscs as in all other marine creatures. Every species has its own temperature range most suitable for its spawning. As the water warms up towards that temperature the eggs and sperm ripen and when the right temperature is reached the shedding of the eggs and sperm begins. A few of the more advanced individuals start the process and then the others follow so that it quickly spreads throughout the whole colony.

Class 6—Cephalopoda (octopus, cuttlefish, squids, the pearly nautilus, the paper nautilus or argonaut). These are the most highly developed of all the molluscs. They have broken away from the substratum, from the rocks, sand or mud of the sea bottom, to become highly mobile, active and predatory. Some, like the squid and cuttle are pelagic, that is, they spend all their lives swimming actively near the surface. Others, like the octopus, are rock and bottom haunting creatures, but still mobile and active. From their appearance it is at first difficult to imagine how the cephalopods can be derived from the mollusc plan. Neverthe-

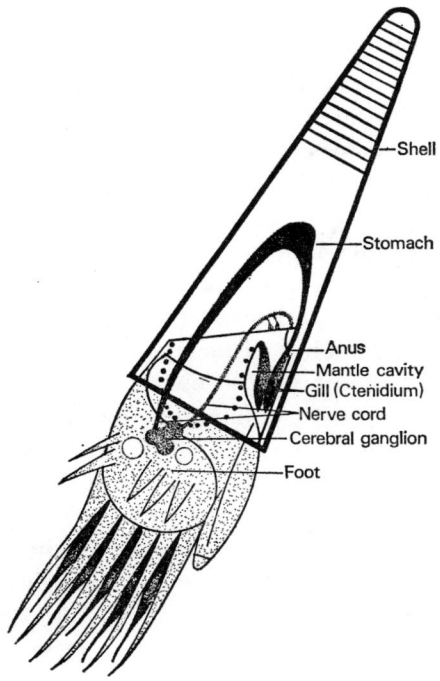

Fig. 8

Diagram of a generalized Cephalopod (Squid, Cuttle or Octopus)

less, the plan is still there. The body has become drawn out (Fig. 8) into a conical pointed dunce's cap with the shell perched like a thimble on the apex of it. The intestine has become a long narrow inverted U with the mouth and anus relatively close to one another, but no torsion has taken place and the anus remains ventral, not dorsal as it is in prosobranch gastropods. The mantle cavity is greatly reduced and forms a small space at the lower forward end of the animal under the head, a position really basal to the cone-shaped body. The foot forms a tube through which water, drawn into the cavity laterally, can be suddenly and violently expelled so that the animal can propel itself backwards at great speed for short distances by jet propulsion. Another part of the foot surrounds the head (Fig. 8) and forms a crown of tentacles, eight in the octopus and ten in the cuttle and squid. These are armed with suckers and, in the tropical mid-ocean squids, the suckers may have horny hooks in the middle of them. The long parallel scratches which sperm whales bear on the sides of their heads bear witness to many a painful meal. The cephalopod head is large and round and has well developed eyes which do not differ very greatly in structure, and so, one must suppose, in efficacy, from those of vertebrates.

All the cephalopods are carnivorous and voracious. The octopus lives on crabs and other crustacea, and the cuttle and squid mainly on fish. They dismember their food with their tentacles and then chew it up by means of a pair of horny jaws inside the head shaped very much like the upper and lower beak of a parrot. They have a very highly developed cerebral nerve ganglion which is believed to have something of the attributes of a brain. Stories are frequently told about these creatures, especially about the octopus, which seem to show that they have some sort of power of choice if not of reasoning. Most of these stories may be taken with a grain of salt, though there may be some truth in some of them. For instance, the octopus has been reported to use dead fish as bait in order to attract the crabs on which it feeds. One octopus was fed oysters but could not open them and left them for crabs which were easier to deal with. Next time it was offered oysters it refused them, having apparently learnt that it could not cope with them. All cephalopods secrete a dark dye, the sepia, from a gland in the mantle cavity. This they squirt into the water when alarmed so as to make a camouflage cloud. Being otherwise defenceless their chief defences are escape and concealment and it had always been supposed that this was the purpose of the sepia cloud. One observer, however, has noticed that the sepia cloud stays as a compact dark, almost solid, mass for quite a long time before diffusing into a cloud, meanwhile

Plate 1. Coat-of-mail shell (*Acanthochitona crinita*). *Photo: M. A. Wilson.*

Plate 2.
Small and
rough
periwinkles
(*Littorina
neritoides* and
L. saxatilis)
together in
cracks in a
rock cliff
near the high
water mark:
North
Cornwall.
*Photo:
Douglas P.
Wilson, FRPS.*

the animal darts away. From this it seems possible that the animal may use the cloud as a kind of decoy, escaping while leaving a model of itself behind. Squids and cuttles have another method of concealment available to them in the capacity rapidly to change the colour of their skin so as to tone with the background.

In cephalopods the sexes are separate and the female deposits large round eggs on the bottom in capsules, guarding them and blowing water over them until the young appear as little replicas of their parents. In some cases the sexes copulate, in others the male transfers the sperm in packets, called 'spermatophores', to one of his tentacles which is specially modified to receive them. The specially modified portion then breaks off and floats about in the sea until a female takes hold of it.

In chalk formations, and in clay and limestone rocks two hundred million years old in Dorset, the Midlands and Yorkshire, we find the fossil remains of chambered shells, some straight and some coiled, which once belonged to an abundant and widespread race of cephalopods. It would seem that they were at that time the dominant animals in those seas (see pp. 156–159). Some of the coiled ones, known as ammonites, may be as big as the wheels of a motor lorry. Today there are still small rare cuttlefish, living in deep tropical waters, which have a coiled, chambered shell in the apex of a cone-shaped body (*Spirula*). In the young animal this shell is exposed but later becomes completely enveloped in an overfold of the skin of the mantle. The only modern living cephalopod which has an external shell is the beautiful pearly nautilus of tropical seas. It occupies a group by itself among the cephalopods. Its exquisite, coiled, pearly shell is divided into a series of chambers by thin partitions (Fig. 9a) and the animal grows by periodic jumps at each of which it moves forward in its shell and secretes a wall behind itself, so that its house comes to consist of a series of semicircular chambers of increasing size arranged in a spiral. In tropical waters there is also the paper nautilus or argonaut (*Argonauta*) in which only the female produces a kind of shell. It is not a house but an egg case and even lovelier than the shell of the pearly utilus, made of a very fine, papery, calcareous material, coiled and sculptured but quite

3

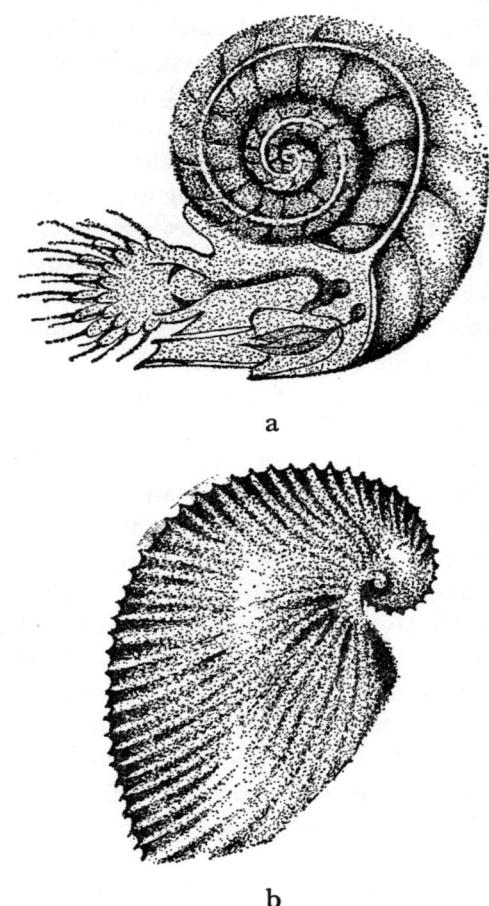

a

b

Fig. 9

A. The Chambered or Pearly Nautilus: *Nautilus pompilius*, diagram-matic. B. Shell of the female Paper Nautilus or Argonaut: *Argonauta argo* × ¼ nat. size approx.

hollow and not chambered (Fig. 9b). It is secreted by two of the tentacle arms of the female. They hold the shell in place as a receptacle for the eggs but the animal does not live inside it. The male argonaut is very small, much smaller than the female, and does not make a shell at all.

None of our northern octopuses, squids or cuttles has a shell at all in the true sense. The cuttle forms a chalky 'pen' which you may often find washed up on the beach and which used to be ground up and used for blotting powder. In the living animal it lies along the back and is not visible from the outside, being entirely overgrown by the mantle. The squid has a thin, membranous horny plate in the same position, also invisible in the living animal. The octopus has no shell at all and its body is a soft, flabby bag unsupported by any skeleton.

By far the greatest number of shells which are likely to make up any collection therefore come from the two great classes of molluscs, the gastropods (limpets and coiled shells) and the lamellibranchs (bivalves). The Loricata and Scaphopoda are comparitively small classes, one found on rocks and the other in sand or mud in fairly deep water.

There are over 70,000 species of molluscs known to science and the number is increasing every year as new ones are discovered. In the tropics their shells achieve a beauty and fantasy of form and colour which we cannot match in our northern seas. As is usual among all animals and plant species, both living and fossil, whether in the sea or on land, the tropics show an immense variety of forms, shapes and patterns, evidence of the ebullience of life in warm climates, while in the colder latitudes there is less variety but a vastly larger number of individuals of each species. Although the numbers of different kinds of shells found around our coasts are comparatively small they are nevertheless so great (there are more than 370 species of gastropods and 180 species of bivalves) that in a short book it is not possible to do more than indicate what sort of shells you may expect to find on what sort of territory.

There are, of course, other sorts of shells in the sea besides those formed by the molluscs, but they really lie outside the orbit

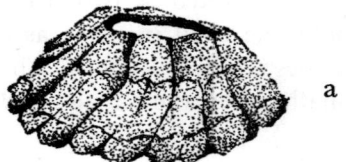

a

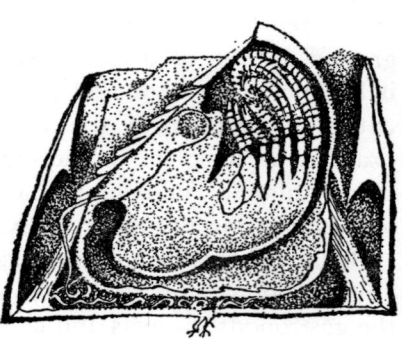

b

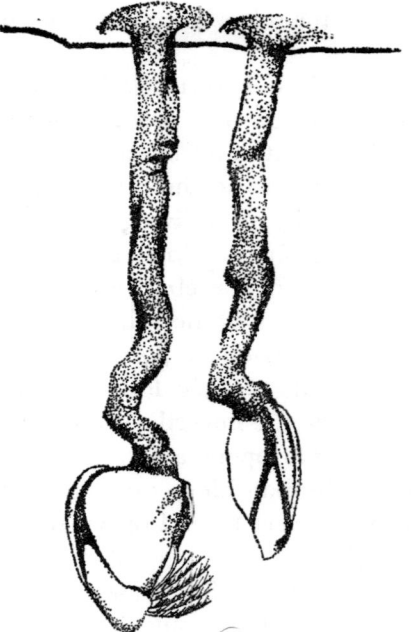

c

Fig. 10 : Barnacles

A. The Acorn barnacle : *Balanus balanoides*, side view × 4 nat. size approx.

B. The Acorn barnacle, vertical section, diagrammatic

C. Stalked barnacles *Lepas anatifera* × ½ nat. size approx.

of the collector. For instance, there are the tiny calcareous houses built by the acorn barnacle which any visitor to the seashore knows. The barnacle is a small crustacean which in early life fixes itself to the rock by its head and then secretes a box of limy

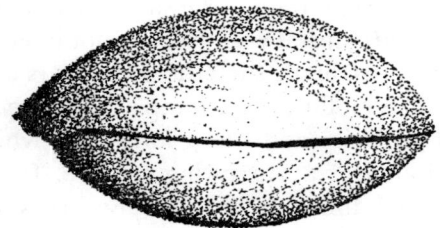

Fig. 11

A Brachiopod or Lamp shell: *Terebratula* sp. × 3 nat. size approx.

plates around itself (Fig. 10a). The box is made of six plates, which fuse together to form an encircling wall, and four which form a movable trap door. The inmate can open these when the water covers its home and shut them again, enclosing a bubble of air, when the house is left high and dry. The barnacle itself lives all its life fixed upside down furiously paddling with its legs in order to draw water into its house. It is a suspension feeder and filters off the suspended matter in the water with the bristles on its six pairs of legs (Fig. 10b).

We have four different species of rock barnacles on our shores. They are all small but in the tropics rock barnacles an inch high may be found. Rock barnacles are said to be 'sessile' (seated). They live pressed close against the rock surface, but there are other barnacles, which may be found on the undersides of driftwood and baulks of timber, or even on boats that have been afloat for a long time without a coating of anti-fouling paint. These are the stalked barnacles, which are much the same as the sessile ones except for a long fleshy stalk, sometimes as much as six inches in length, which is what has become of the animal's fixed head (Fig. 10c). The house in which the animal lives is flattened and not ring-shaped.

Another kind of shell which might perhaps be mentioned is the lamp shell. Lamp shells belong to a group of animals of uncertain relationships, quite different from the Mollusca, known as the Brachiopoda (Fig. 11). They mostly live in deep water and, though they look like bivalve molluscs, they have actually only a superficial resemblance to them. The shell may be limy or horny and the two valves are dorsal and ventral, not lateral like those of the lamellibranchs. Inside the shell the body bears no resemblance whatever to that of a mollusc. One lamp shell (*Lingula*) lives in the mud of tropical estuaries and has a long stalk which looks very much like the siphon of a burrowing bivalve. In fact it has no inhalent or exhalent function but merely serves to attach the animal to its burrow. In Ordovician and Silurian times, 450 to 500 million years ago, the Brachiopods were a numerous and predominant race of animals (see p. 160), but they have since diminished to their present position of relative unimportance.

2

COLLECTING

THE SYSTEMATIC collecting of sea shells needs a great deal of care and thought and involves much more than just grubbing around on the beach.

The mollusc in its shell is a living animal and is therefore influenced by all the factors which make up a living animal's environment, such as the supply of the right kind of food, the supply of oxygen for breathing, the availability of a suitable substratum, the presence of the right conditions for breeding, the presence of enemies. If you wander along the beach just picking up shells at random you will only find the broken and cast-off houses of the living animal, all removed from their natural position. They will all be broken or damaged and often only the single valves of bivalves will be found. You must collect the complete living animal and for that purpose you must be able to find the place where it lives. You must know what to expect to find and where. It is also useful to know why. For this you must make a study of the animal's environment and understand the factors that influence it and cause it to be where it is. The shapes of shells are related to the way they live, to their habits, and to the animal's food. Their colours are related to their background and often vary greatly in the same species.

Precise details about every specimen you collect are very important. The date, the time, the state of the tide and a brief note about the locality (whether on rock, stones, sand, mud, etc.), should all be written down. Colour notes are also important for the reasons given above and because it may be that when someone comes to look at your collection in fifty years' time the colours of many of the shells will have faded and changed.

A large collection of sea shells properly annotated is of

39

considerable commercial value, and the more complete it is, of course, the greater its value. Specimens of shells properly labelled and annotated are naturally of much more value than those about which no or insufficient details have been recorded. They are also of much greater scientific interest. There are dealers in sea shells both in Britain and America. One of the most famous in London is Eaton's Shell Shop, 16 Manette Street, Soho, w.1. An American publisher, van Nostrand, now publishes a catalogue giving the market prices of a wide range of sea shells, and some of the rarer ones, such as sinistral specimens of normally dextral conch shells, are marked as high as $200. Perhaps the most celebrated shell in the world is the beautiful involuted coiled gastropod, nearly six inches high with an almost opalescent pink and gold sheen, the Glory of the Sea (*Conus gloriamaris*), of which there is a specimen in the Natural History Museum at South Kensington. The earliest known specimens in the eighteenth century were believed to come from the shores of New Guinea and until the middle of the nineteenth century there were only two or three specimens known. For over two centuries the Glory of the Sea was the rarest and most coveted shell in the world. There is a story, now known to be apocryphal, that at one time there were only two specimens in collections. When one of them came up for sale by auction a famous Dutch collector bought it, outbidding all his rivals, and, when he had got possession of it, crushed it beneath his heel, exclaiming 'Now my specimen is the only one'. Today there are more than forty specimens in existence and the Glory of the Sea is believed to be fairly common in the waters around New Guinea and New Britain. But it is still highly enough esteemed for an American collector to pay $2,000 for a specimen as recently as 1964. Other shells for which high prices were paid in the eighteenth and early nineteenth centuries, but which are now very much less valuable because less rare, are the Precious Wentletrap (*Scalaria pretiosa*), from eastern tropical waters, and the Matchless Cone (*Conus cedonulli*). The latter is now known to comprise three separate species and conchologists do not recognize *C. cedonulli* as a true species at all.

It seems hard to believe but some people, especially in the last century, actually built up their collections entirely by buying from dealers. How much more satisfying and soothing to the spirit to go hunting along the beach yourself, hunting out these jewels where they lurk glowing in dark crevices, or digging them out of their sandy or muddy lairs.

The molluscs live in every environment from the great depths of the sea (2,900 fathoms) up to mountain tops 15,000 feet above sea level. Yet their true home is the sea shore and the shallow sunlit water just below low tide. From there out to about fifty fathoms they reach their greatest abundance and variety. They become less abundant towards the high tide mark and below the low tide mark slowly thin out over the ocean floor down to a hundred fathoms.

It is not very difficult to understand why this is. Between the tide marks conditions, not only for molluscs but for all the creatures of the sea, become increasingly hazardous as you go up the shore from the low to the high tide mark. Living things in this zone have to be able to accustom themselves to wide variations in all the factors governing their lives with terrestrial influences gaining the ascendancy towards the high tide mark and marine influences towards the low. Between the level of the low water neap tides and that of the low water springs is the zone where life generally is most prolific, for here the water is brightly lit by the sun and well oxygenated by being constantly stirred by the wash of waves and tides. Temperatures are most constant along this zone and the risk of being dried up twice daily by the receding tide is least. Here, therefore, at extreme low tide competition among living creatures is most intense, the supply of food most abundant and assured. Many shore animals have a wide range of tolerance of variations in these factors, can withstand being dried up for long periods and subsist on diminished supplies of oxygen. But the majority is less well adapted to extremes. The zone of extreme low tides is therefore the happiest hunting ground for anyone collecting anything, shells included. Low spring tides take place at the full and the new moons, that is once a fortnight, but the lowest spring tides of all are those which take place at the equinoxes in mid-March and mid-September. It is then that rocks or sand flats or mud banks are exposed which are covered at all other times of the year. You behold strange shapes which you have never seen before with tresses of shining strap weed and great holdfasts gripping the rocks full of minute treasures. This is the time when the collector should be down on the rocks with his swimming trunks and rope soles (very important), his goggling mask and breathing tube. Cold work in March, however, and I recommend the September spring tides for this! A bright moonlit night is the best time for collecting shells. Take an electric torch and you will see that all the rock-dwelling molluscs are out from their hiding places foraging for food, and the burrowers are up, at or near the surface.

Very little apparatus is needed for collecting shells. I recommend carrying a wicker collecting basket with a central handle, which your forearm can go through, divided into a number of rectangular compartments able to contain screw-topped jars of up to 1 lb. capacity. Ideally the bottles should have glass tops with rubber washers and brass screw bands round the top ('Kilner' jars). As many glass, or perhaps better polythene, tubes as possible, of as many different sizes as possible, should also be carried in the basket. The reason for all this paraphernalia is that after an hour or so of collecting one cannot possibly remember what has been collected where. Specimens should therefore be labelled right on the spot with full details of time and habitat. Each specimen, as it is collected and labelled, can then be placed with its label in a suitable jar or tube. If you wish to preserve permanently the entire animal a little 5 per cent formalin (commercial 40 per cent, diluted about eight times), enough to cover the specimen, should be placed in the bottle or tube. Tubes can be sealed temporarily with corks while collecting but not permanently if the specimens are in fluid because corks leak (see p. 47). Some collectors recommend cardboard boxes. These are good enough but they will almost certainly disintegrate before very long for remember that when you are collecting on the shore everything gets wet. The sea is wet, your clothes and hands will be wet, and it may be raining. Cardboard boxes, however, are excellent for storing shells dry at home.

Wherever you are collecting, whether on rocks, sand or mud, or when using a goggling mask and breathing tube, never neglect to wear something on your feet. Many shells and marine animals have sharp edges and spines which may inflict exceedingly unpleasant wounds liable to turn septic. On rocks sea urchins have especially dangerous spines which break off in the skin and cause great pain. In sand and mud sea urchins and weaver fish with dangerous spines lie hidden beneath the surface, and in mud fan mussels have large upwardly directed curved edges like knives. Personally I found a pair of canvas base-ball boots with rubber soles absolutely invaluable. They protect not only the soles but the ankles also and have ridged rubber soles which do not slip.

Correct labelling is one of the most important and neglected of the collector's duties. To begin with every label should be written clearly in dark pencil since other people will probably want to read it long after the collector is dead and forgotten. If ink is used make sure that it is a good one that is waterproof and does not run. The label should be placed inside the tube or bottle with the specimen. Never try to stick on sticky labels because they always come off. Labels should be made of pulpless paper if possible (I.C.I. make a brand known as 'Cobex').

It is wise to allot to every separate locality, date and time of collecting a separate collecting number. Suppose, for example, you collect near the low tide mark among rocks covered with wrack weed in Sandy Cove at 11.30 a.m. on 18th May 1966. You may allot to that occasion a number, say No. 1. If then you move on to another place along the beach immediately afterwards, give that occasion the next number, say No. 2. If you go back to the position of No. 1. at 4.00 p.m. (easier to call it 1600) the following day, give that another number, say No. 3. Conditions will not be the same as they were yesterday. The state of the tide and the weather anyhow will be different. Thus give a serial number to all your occasions of collecting, no matter how close together in time or locality. There is, after all, no risk of running out of numbers. The numbers of 'stations', as these collecting points may be called, made by the major expeditions to the Antarctic or to the Great Barrier Reef ran into thousands. You can then keep a log book recording against each collecting or 'station' number the date, time, state of the tide, type of locality and any other condition you like to mention. The label itself may merely carry the collecting or 'station' number perhaps with the date, time and place, thus:

> St. No. 47   18. v. 66
> By hand.   1430–1630,
>   Sandy Cove, Trebarwith,
>   Cornwall.
> On rocks, among bladder wrack. Half tide.

On the back of the label you may write some brief description of the specimen—'Cowrie white three brownish spots on back'.

You should also keep a catalogue of specimens with a catalogue number for every one. This should appear on the label in the final display case.

The entry in the collector's log book should read like this:

> St. No. 47   18. v. 66.   1430–1630
> By hand   Sandy Cove, Trebarwith,
>   Cornwall. Half neap tide,
>   going out. Cloudy. Rocks
>   at western end with Fucus
>   and corallines. Castle Rock
>   bg 035°.
> Cowrie—Cat. No. 382
> Slit limpet—Cat. No. 462
> Rosy slit limpet—Cat. No. 463.

Further details about the specimens themselves can be entered in the catalogue, thus:

> Cat. No. 382 European   *Trivia monacha* White with
> cowrie   three brownish spots on
>   the back. St. 47.

There should also be a card index of specimens (with catalogue and station numbers) arranged by classes, subclasses, orders, suborders, families, genera and species. Each species should have a card to itself. For both station log and catalogue Ryman's loose-leaf folder ('New Albemarle') is very useful.

Every collector develops his own technique and the above is merely a suggestion for the collector who goes searching for his own shells. Many collectors, however, receive shells from others both at home and abroad. Needless to say every specimen received from another collector should be catalogued and labelled with a catalogue number and details of when and where collected and from whom received. Thus the catalogue entry might read:

Cat. No.	Specimen	Collector	Date recd.	Locality	Remarks
*M87	Mauritius cowrie *Cypraea mauritiana*	J. Christophe	25.ix.63	Poudre d'Or Mauri-tuis	Coral lagoon

*Mauritius

So far we have been simply scrambling about the rocks, or digging along the low tide mark in sand or mud, but a great many molluscs live in shallow water below the lowest spring tides and are never uncovered at all. Many of these may be collected with a boat towing a naturalist's or a conical dredge. The naturalist's dredge is a bag of netting with its mouth attached to a heavy rectangular iron frame about two feet wide with outwardly curved upper and lower flanges (Fig. 12a) which bite into the sea bottom. The mouth of the dredge has two iron vertical side pieces on which are threaded the Y-shaped yokes with terminal eyes for hauling the apparatus. One yoke is longer than the other. The terminal eye of the longer one is shackled to the hauling rope while that of the shorter is lashed with twine to the eye of its fellow, not shackled to the hauling line. Thus if any undue strain comes on the dredge during hauling the twine snaps, the yokes fall apart and the dredge itself is not damaged. A sheet of canvas may be placed under the bag of netting to make the dredge run over the bottom smoothly.

The naturalist's dredge is made of netting and lets through the finest material. For collecting fine sand or mud from the

bottom the conical dredge (Fig. 12b) is much more efficient.
It is a cone of stiff canvas with a circular iron lip which also digs
into the bottom. This takes a convenient sample of both coarse
and fine material which may be taken home and sifted through

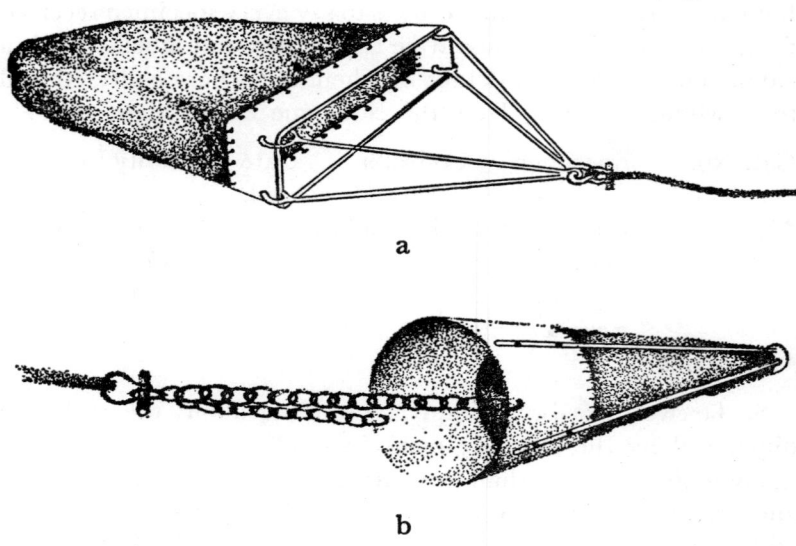

a

b

Fig. 12

A. Naturalist's dredge   B. Conical dredge

at leisure. When dredging from a boat a length of line equal to
about three times the estimated depth of the water should be let
out. Make sure that the dredge is actually on the bottom by
feeling the vibration of the hauling rope. Do not let the boat go
too fast for that will either lose the dredge if it strikes an obstruc-
tion under water or will lift it off the bottom so that it catches
nothing.

The naturalist's dredge will bring up large stones and the holdfasts of weeds with shells attached to them. These tough strong
holdfasts always shelter an abundance of life of all sorts. But for
hunting over rocks below low tide a goggling mask and breathing

tube or a diver's helmet must be used. It is useful to take down several cotton or canvas bags with slip openings. These can be slung around the waist to receive specimens as you collect them, but remember to label them and place them in their separate tubes or jars as soon as you surface.

When collecting on rocks look in all the sheltered places, in cracks and crevices, under stones and among the fronds of seaweed. Holdfasts should be cut off and shaken into a bucket of sea water. If they are kept in the bucket of water for a while the gradual warming of the water will make the inmates come out of their hiding places. A glass-bottomed box is also very useful for looking into rock pools, especially when the surface is furrowed by the wind.

If you wish to collect the animals entire with the soft parts keep them in tubes of 5 per cent formalin, properly labelled of course. Take care that the formalin is neutral for if it is at all acid it will in time dissolve away the calcareous parts such as the molluscs' shells. For this purpose keep the formalin in a jar with calcium carbonate (marble or chalk) sprinkled over the bottom. A small chip of marble may be kept in the tube with the specimen. For permanent preservation remove the corks from the tubes and plug each tube with a bung made of cotton wool wrapped in two thicknesses of tissue paper. Keep the tubes plugged in this way all together in a large screw-topped jar filled with 5 per cent formalin. They will then be safe for ever from evaporation. No cork is leak-proof and tubes standing on a shelf and sealed only with corks become quite dry in course of time.

Most people, however, prefer to make collections of dry shells. It is on the shell that the animal's environment has impressed itself so as to produce that bewildering variety of form and colour, and it is in the shell that the wonder and beauty of molluscs reside. The soft body of, say, a marine gastropod is much the same over a wide range of types and, preserved in formalin or alcohol, it is not a very lovely object, resembling a piece of india-rubber.

The first task when you get the spoils of your foray home is to get the animals out of their shells. For lamellibranchs the best way to do this is to place the animal in warm fresh water. Lack of oxygen will make it gape so that you can get a knife in and cut the adductor muscles. The rest of the body can then be scooped out. Gastropods, especially the larger ones, can be extracted by placing them in fresh water and bringing them slowly to the boil. Never plunge them direct into boiling water because this may split the shell. The body can then be drawn out with a pin or a skewer in the good old winkle style. Alternatively, the large gastropods may be buried in earth or sand and the body left to rot, though this may take several weeks. Or they may be exposed on a shelf in the sun so that blow fly larvae and ants can do the job. They will do it very efficiently but I recommend that the mortuary shelf be as far as possible from the house and the neighbours because in a day or two the specimens will become very high indeed.

When the animals have been removed the shells should be washed in warm water with a fairly soft brush and then placed in dilute household bleach for a few hours. After that they should be rinsed, dried and coated with thin varnish, also using a soft brush.

When the shells have been emptied and cleaned an attempt should be made to arrive at the scientific name of each one. This classification may be left to this stage because it is solely on the characters of the shell that molluscs are classified into families, genera and species. You yourself can place them in their families, genera and species with patience and perserverance, perhaps in consultation with other shell experts. It may take a long time but you will find it a fascinating and time-consuming exercise, similar to doing a Chinese puzzle. You should make use of one of the published keys which have been drawn up by conchologists who are already experts and have over the years trained themselves in exactly the same way, by observation and experience. In many cases the field in which experts in animal or plant classification are trained is quite a narrow one, embracing perhaps only a single subclass or a few suborders. Most scientists specialize in their own favourite groups and the number of collectors who can be said to be expert in the Mollusca as a whole is very small.

Plate 3. Flat periwinkles (*Littorina littoralis*) on knotted wrack. *Photo: Douglas P. Wilson, FRPS.*

Plate 4.
Common
periwinkles
(*Littorina
littorea*) on
rocks amid
seaweeds.
*Photo:
Douglas P.
Wilson, FRPS.*

Identification keys for all plants and animals, living or fossil, proceed by a process of elimination, working down from phylum to class, from class to subclass, order to suborder, thence to family, genus and species. With a little practice you will soon be able to place your specimens direct into the sub-class or order, even into the family and genus, and then proceed with the key down to the species. The use of a key, however, requires a technical familiarity with the various terms used to describe characters and features of the specimen's anatomy or structure on which the classification is based. In the case of the mollusca you will need to familiarize yourself with the technical terms which are applied to the various parts of the shell and which you will find constantly used in the keys. For convenience a list of some of these is given in Appendix II.

As an exercise it is a good idea at first to try yourself out with shells whose identification you are already certain of, say the common dog whelk(*Nucella lapillus*), the common cockle (*Cerastoderma (Cardium) edule*), the common mussel (*Mytilus edulis*), and the common limpet (*Patella vulgata*), and run them down with a key, starting with the phylum and ending with the species. This will familiarize you with the way the key works. You will learn to do this fairly quickly, but as you become acquainted with the various groups you may find that there is a good deal of disagreement among the authors of various keys both about the characters and the names of the various groups, especially about the finer points which distinguish species from one another. Scientists concerned with classification are of two kinds, the 'whole hoggers' and the 'hair splitters'. The former tend to lump species together under the heading of comparatively few characters while the latter like to build up an elaborate classification based on a large number of minute differences. You may take your choice which you will be yourself.

In Appendix III a short list is given of recommended guides to the commoner British Mollusca, some of which have keys.

In order to display your collection the shells should be stuck on to cards or kept in cardboard boxes, perhaps with glass tops. It is best to use both, keeping the cards with the shells stuck to

4

them with a touch of Canada balsam, inside the boxes. The boxes may then be arranged in drawers in a cabinet. Each card should carry the popular and scientific name of the shell and its station and catalogue number so that all details about the specimen can be easily referred to. Do not stick labels on to the shells themselves and do not have shells lying about loose in drawers because they will knock against each other and be damaged every time you open or shut the drawer.

3

ON THE ROCKS

THE SEA SHORE is the strip of territory between the tide marks where the sea and the land dispute with each other for mastery. On the landward side it is bounded by the highest spring tide mark and on its seaward side by the level of the lowest springs. Above the highest tide mark there still remains a zone which is reached only by spray from breaking waves at the highest tides and here some of the toughest, yet truly shore-inhabiting, plants and animals live, well adapted to long exposure and desiccation. From the level of the highest spring tides to that of the average high tides is the zone which is called the 'upper shore'. The 'middle shore' extends from the average high tide to the average low tide level and the 'lower shore' thence to the level of the lowest springs. Beyond that we come to the shallow water or 'sublittoral' zone which is never uncovered and where the collector must either go out in a boat or put on his swimming trunks and diving mask.

The sea shore, of course, varies very greatly in character, but broadly we can distinguish the shore made of rocks with pools between them, the shore made of sand—soft or firm, coarse or fine—and the shore made of mud, usually in the upper parts of estuaries where the water is shallow, calm and brackish. Each of these has its own characteristic population of animals and plants but, of course, they mingle and merge with one another to a very great extent as rocks merge and mingle with sand and sand with mud. Each population is specially adapted to cope with the peculiar problems which life in its habitat presents to it. Perhaps also we should mention the purely shingle beach. It is constantly pounded by waves and shifted by tides and currents, and is comparatively barren of life, certainly of shells, owing to

51

the grinding action of the stones against one another. Finally, in the sublittoral zone the character of the population, as a rule much denser and more prolific than on the exposed shore, will depend on the type of bottom. This, again, may be rocky, sandy or muddy.

On the rocks, and on the rocky shore generally, the conditions of life fluctuate between wide extremes and are far less uniform than on sandy or muddy shores where, by burrowing into the substratum, animals may escape into a dark, clammy world of their own. But even there life is not without certain hazards. On the rocks the chief problems animals have to contend with are how to cling on and resist the battering of the waves and the swirl of currents, and how to withstand long periods of drying up with sudden and wide changes of temperature and oxygen supply. In the sand and mud, on the other hand, the chief problems are how to remain anchored in a constantly shifting substratum and how to keep contact with the world above while lying buried.

From the high tide mark to the low conditions on the rocky shore grade slowly from the terrestrial to the marine. The terrestrial conditions of rapidly changing temperature and salinity, bright light, diminished oxygen supply and mechanical battering get less and less down to the lowest tides and the shallow offshore waters of the sublittoral zone. Many of the plants and animals that live fastened to rocks are adapted to withstand wide variations in all these conditions and may, therefore, like the acorn barnacle for instance, be found widely distributed, living equally happily everywhere from above the highest tide mark to below the lowest. But many are in varying degrees less adaptable and tend to sort themselves out along the rocky shore in zones or bands according to their several powers of resistance to exposure, temperature and salinity change, oxygen lack, mechanical battering, and so on.

The zonation or banding of living things on the rocky shore is noticeable at a glance in the case of the larger seaweeds. Above the high tide mark, where there is much fresh water, we come first to the green slime weed (*Enteromorpha*), which can withstand long periods of drying up during which it turns white and stiff. On the shore itself, in pools which may often be diluted with fresh water down to those often freshened by the sea, we find a darker green, rather hairy-looking weed (*Cladophora ruprestris*), and then comes the filmy green sea lettuce (*Ulva lactuca*) which is found all over the rocks, but always where there is some exposure but not too much drying up.

The so-called brown seaweeds, which are actually not brown but green, include those masses and cushions of wrack weed which clothe the rocks like thick tresses. They are all very sharply zoned, each separate species occupying its own special zone down to the low tide mark. All these thick masses of weed have a very useful function in the economy of the sea shore since they give shelter among and on their fronds, and in their branching 'roots' or holdfasts, to a great multitude of tiny animals, including molluscs. In addition they break the force of the waves and keep the temperature of the shallow waters and pools even by giving shade and promoting evaporation.

Below the low tide mark in the sublittoral zone is the habitat of the great throng weeds and the strap and ribbon weeds. These often have wide fronds many feet in length, frequently to be found cast up on the beach, and large branching, disc-like or bulbous holdfasts.

The shell life on the rocky shore also shows zonation in varying degrees similar to that shown by the seaweeds but much less striking. While many molluscs, such as the common limpet and the common mussel, are evenly distributed from the high tide mark to the low there are others which are confined to comparatively narrow bands. There are limpets and mussels which are only found at extreme low tide and others again which are confined to the sublittoral zone.

Zonation on the rocks is best illustrated among molluscs by the periwinkles (Pls. 2, 3, 4) which are the commonest of all the marine snail-like gastropods. You will find them scattered abundantly on the faces of the rocks but more often crowded into damp crevices, sheltering from the waves, or on the fronds of wrack weeds.

The small periwinkle (*Littorina neritoides*—Pl. 2) is a small, smooth, pointed, dark shell, usually less than one-fifth of an inch in height. It crowds into crevices along the high tide mark and often inside the empty cases of barnacles. It feeds on lichens and can resist drying up for long periods.

The rough periwinkle (*L. saxatilis*—Pl. 2) is somewhat larger (a quarter of an inch to half an inch) with a rough ribbed shell, red or black, but sometimes white or yellow, and a comparatively wide first whorl covered with wrinkles. It occupies a second strip of shore from about the 'splash' zone (the zone reached only by the spray of breaking waves at the highest tides) to about half tide level. It is to be found in less exposed places than the small periwinkle because it is sensitive to exposure and, in order to avoid this risk, produces its young fully formed from inside the mantle cavity. It is the only periwinkle to have adopted this method of breeding to avoid the risk of exposing its young to desiccation.

The flat periwinkle (*L. littoralis*—Pl. 3) is confined to the zone of the bladder and knotted wracks and is often to be found crawling on the fronds of one or the other. It is very variable in colour, yellow, orange, green or dark red, brown or purple, and sometimes spirally striped with dark colours on a yellow or green ground. It has a flat-topped and not pointed spire.

The common winkle (*Littorina littorea*—Pl. 4) lives between the high neap tide level and the lowest springs on every kind of substratum from exposed rock to soft sand or mud. It can tolerate almost fresh water and is gathered commercially in large numbers in the English east coast estuaries. It is the largest of our winkles with a pointed spire which may be as much as one inch high. It is dark grey, black, or red with a rough surface in smaller, younger shells but a smooth surface in older ones.

Periwinkles are easily detachable from the rocks but, withdrawn into their smooth, rounded houses, they can be bowled and trundled about by the waves without damage. They can resist drying up by glueing the edges of their shells to the rocks with a film of mucus. This dries and leaves the shell gummed to the rock, usually upside down, with the animal completely withdrawn inside it.

Related to the periwinkles is the banded chink shell (*Lacuna vincta*) which occurs with them on the lower shore among weeds. It is usually yellow with reddish brown bands and has a conspicuous hole or umbilicus on the underside within the whorls.

The top shells (Pl. 5, Fig. 13) belong to the gastropod family Trochidae which includes the tropical shells from which pearl buttons are made. They are so called because they have all to some degree a triangular outline like a child's toy top upside down. The last whorl is flattened so that the shell has a flat base and there is a well defined umbilicus within the whorls. Our top shells are all very much smaller than the pearl button shells of the tropics which may attain a height of four inches, but they are all distinguished by a pearly sheen caused by the pearly or nacreous layer of the shell showing through as the outer layers wear thin.

Like the periwinkles the top shells occupy fairly well marked zones on the rocks. They are herbivorous and are usually found on clean exposed surfaces of rock or browsing on weeds. The best known is the common or painted top (*Calliostoma zizyphinum*— Pl. 5) which has a very triangular outline, straight sides and flat base. It is the largest of our top shells, yellow, pink, or white with red streaks. It occurs at very low tide on our southern and western coasts.

The thick top (*Gibbula lineata*—Fig. 13a) is a large, rather more rounded shell, grey or greenish, with a very pearly aperture. It is about the same size as the painted top and occupies a zone in the middle shore along our western coasts. The very much commoner grey top (*G. cineraria*—Fig. 13b) is about half the size of the other two and occupies the middle and lower shores. It is grey in colour with narrow dark stripes.

The flat or purple top (*G. umbilicalis*) is similar to the grey top but greenish with broader stripes. It occupies the middle shore and the upper part of the lower shore.

The yellow pheasant shell (*Tricolia pullus*—Fig. 13c) is related to the top shells but is smaller and rounder, about one-third of an inch in height. It has a calcareous operculum while the top shells have horny ones. It is quite common at low tide along our south-western coasts.

The largest and commonest of the snail-like coiled gastropods to be found cruising about the rocks are the whelks (Frontispiece, Pl. 6, Fig. 14). They have thick, sharply pointed shells with a large siphon projecting upwards through a distinct canal or notch in the margin

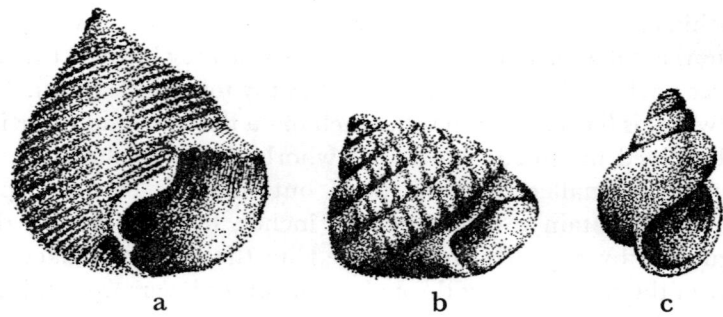

a   b   c

Fig. 13: Top shells

A. The Thick Top shell: *Gibbula lineata* × 1¼ nat. size approx.
B. The Grey Top shell: *Gibbula cineraria* × 1½ nat. size approx.
c. The Yellow Pheasant shell: *Tricolia pullus* × 4 nat. size approx.

of the aperture. They are fierce carnivorous snails which bore holes in the shells of other molluscs, especially other snails, limpets, mussels and also barnacles. They do this with their drill-like radulae and rasp out the animal inside through the hole. They belong to the family Muricidae which includes the Murex shell (*Murex trunculus*) which lives on the shores of the Mediterranean and gave Tyrian purple to the Phoenicians. This is a dye secreted by a gland in a cavity behind the head. Our whelks too have a similar cavity and gland secreting a dye. That of the common dog whelk becomes greenish on exposure to air and at one time was used in Ireland for dying clothes. The whelks also show a certain amount of zoning in their distribution.

The dog whelk or dog winkle (*Nucella lapillus*—Frontispiece, Pl. 6) is a short, thick shell with numerous spiral ridges. It is variously coloured according to its diet. Whelks which have been feeding on mussels are usually dark while those which have been feeding on acorn barnacles are usually white. The dog whelk much prefers mussels to barnacles and will not attack barnacles until the supply of mussels runs out. Sometimes the shell is banded white and brown, perhaps as a result of a mixed diet, and sometimes it may be yellow, though this colour seems to have something to do with exposure to wave action rather than diet. Dog whelks are very common and widely distributed, usually where there are either barnacles or mussels, and that means practically everywhere about the rocks. They often gather in clusters in crevices where they deposit their egg capsules, each one like a grain of corn standing upright on a stalk.

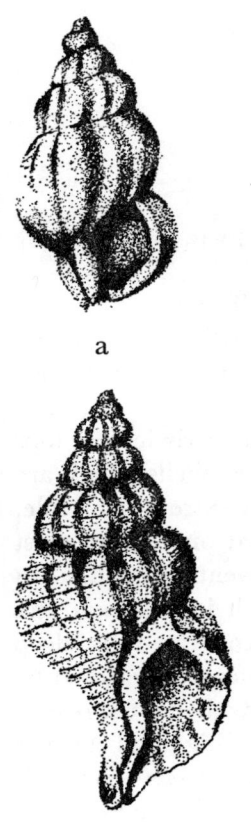

a

b

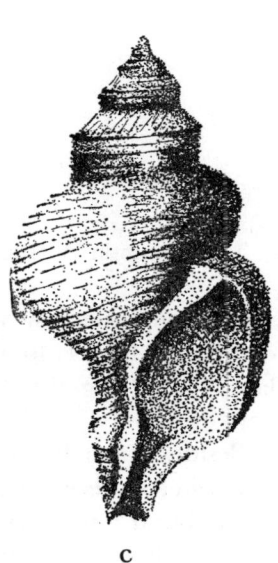

c

d

Fig. 14 : Whelks

A. The Thick-lipped Dog whelk: *Nassarius incrassatus* × 2 nat. size

B. The Netted Dog whelk: *Nassarius reticulatus* × 1½ nat. size approx.

C. The Spindle shell: *Neptunea antiqua* × 1¼ nat. size approx.

D. The Oyster Drill: *Urosalpinx cinerea* × 1 nat. size approx.

Another much smaller whelk, the thick-lipped dog whelk (*Nassarius incrassatus*—Fig. 14a), frequents the lower rocky shore along the low tide mark. Its pointed spire is marked by pronounced vertical ridges and its foot is divided into two distinct tails behind the shell. Another whelk, the netted dog whelk (Fig. 14b), lives on

Fig. 15

The Common Wentletrap: *Clathrus clathrus* × 1¼ nat. size approx.

sand along the low tide mark (see p. 82). The big buckie or common whelk is found mainly offshore and will be mentioned later (p. 92) together with two whelks which are pests of oysters (pp. 93–94).

Besides these bulbous coiled shells like the periwinkles, tops and whelks there are also some tall, thin-spired shells which are to be found low down on the shore, mostly at extreme low tide. One of the largest and most beautiful, indeed one of the most beautiful of all British shells, is the common wentletrap (*Clathrus clathrus*—Fig. 15). It is about one and a half inches high and very narrow, having about fifteen whorls separated by deep sutures. The shell is cream or fawn but the whorls are crossed by raised ridges of pure white. Another tall, narrow shell is the needle shell (*Bittium reticulatum*). It is about half an inch high and covered with network sculpturings (hence the name *reticulatum*—'netted') which in older shells become smoothed down to a large extent.

On our coasts most of these tall thin shells are very small but in the tropics they reach a considerable size and great beauty.

Along the extreme low tide mark on our coasts tiny narrow shells of the family Rissoidae occur, usually on Laminaria weed and in holdfasts. They are usually yellow or yellowish white with brown markings but one (*Barleeia*) is red. A banded one (*Cingula*) is found frequently in empty barnacle cases.

Cowrie shells also grow to a large size and marvellous beauty in the tropics but in our waters there are only two very small ones. The cowries are snails in which the final whorl has enveloped all the others so that the aperture is a narrow slit with crenellated lips. The animal enwraps its entire shell in folds of the mantle tissue so that the outside of the shell is always glossy and highly polished. A short siphon projects in front.

Our comparatively tiny cowries are found on rocks in the Laminarian zone and they seem to be very local in their distribution. They are usually found where there are compound sea-squirts (*Botryllus*) on which they feed and among which they deposit their egg capsules. Our European cowrie (*Trivia monacha* —Pl. 8) is about half an inch long with a white shell crossed by 20 to 25 ribs. It has three brownish spots on its back. The other slightly smaller species (*T. arctica*) has no spots and is less common. It was at one time thought to be merely a variety of the European cowrie.

All these snail shells have a tall spire and not a very pronounced umbilicus. But we have some tiny, flat, almost circular shells, the Skeneopsidae, which are almost like minute coins with a very well marked hole or umbilicus between the whorls. The commonest is the dolphin shell (*Skeneopsis planorbis*), a minute flat coiled shell of four whorls, pale brown or green, common under stones or on weed, but so tiny, about one-sixteenth of an inch in diameter, that it must be searched for very carefully.

In addition to all these coiled shells of the rocky shore there are the limpets (Fig. 16), like Chinese hats, which every visitor to the sea shore knows. They are coiled in early life but develop the conical hat shape as they grow older. They are the most familiar and conspicuous gastropods on the rocks, occupying both exposed and sheltered places. You will notice that in exposed places the limpets are taller and narrower than those which live in sheltered places, in crevices, under weeds or in pools. Here they grow wider and flatter. This is really the opposite of what you would expect but is believed to be due to the fact that in exposed situations the muscles inside the shell will pull down more vigorously and constantly than in sheltered positions so as to anchor the shell more firmly to the rock. They are thus continually being exercised and so, by their greater development, give a higher shape to the shell which accommodates them. If limpets are taken from exposed situations and placed in sheltered ones they flatten out and start to grow wider so that the shape of a hat with a brim is produced.

Limpets feed on the germinating 'sporulae' of seaweeds, the small spores or seeds. You may often notice how each limpet on a rock face has cleared a territory around itself, a patch bare of weeds which it has kept clear during its feeding forays. Limpets do not seem to travel far from their original station in life but tend to occupy a central position in the middle of a territory and make forays in all directions, returning repeatedly to the centre.

The limpet differs from other gastropods in that it has lost its plume-like gill or 'ctenidium' and has developed a ring-like fringe of the mantle made up of thin ciliated platelets within the roof of the mantle cavity beneath the margin of the shell. When the limpet is clamped to its rock enough water is trapped under the margin of the shell for this organ to function as a gill even though the limpet may be exposed for hours.

The limpet's foot is a powerful muscular disc with which the animal fixes itself to the rock surface, forming an extraordinarily close attachment. It is not quite certain just how a limpet does manage to clamp itself so firmly to the rock face but it is believed to be done by filling every minute rugosity and roughness of the rock surface with the muscular flesh of the foot. It used to be thought that the limpet, having applied itself to the rock face, withdrew the foot and created a vacuum underneath it, but this is not now believed to be true. By whatever means it achieves and maintains its grip it is impossible to dislodge a limpet simply by applying pressure. Only a sudden, sharp surprise blow will do the trick.

All limpets start life as males and then become females later on, a state of affairs quite usual in gastropods. Most of the small limpets, therefore, found on the rocks are males and most of the large ones females. They breed very early in the year along our coasts, in January and February, shedding their eggs and sperm into the water. Clouds of minute free-drifting larvae settle down and within a year have grown into limpets about an inch in diameter. As already stated, they do not seem to move a great deal from the spot where the larvae first settle.

The common limpet (*Patella vulgata*—Fig. 16a) is exceedingly abundant everywhere all over the rocks, in both exposed and sheltered places and on stones. It is a brownish, plain conical shell, yellow inside and unstriped. There are, however, two other common limpets (*P. intermedia* and *P. aspera*—Figs. 16b & c) which do not grow so high up exposed shores as does *P. vulgata*. Both of these are smaller and flatter than the common limpet. *P. intermedia* has dark rays on the inner margin of the shell and *P. aspera*, which is flatter than either of the other two, is orange and creamy inside. It is markedly asymmetrical with the apex near the anterior margin of the shell.

The tortoiseshell limpet (*Acmaea tessulata*—Fig. 16d) has brown markings on the shell and the white tortoiseshell limpet (*A. virginea*) is pinkish white. The tortoiseshell limpet is only found on our northern coasts, usually low down on the shore, occasionally fairly high up though never in exposed positions. The white tortoiseshell is common everywhere among Laminaria weed but does not live higher up the shore.

On Laminaria straps and stems, often in holes which it excavates in the tissues of the weed itself, lives the little blue-rayed limpet (*Patina pellucida*—Fig. 16e) which is marked with blue lines and spots.

In addition there are two limpets on our coasts which have perforated shells. The keyhole limpet (*Diodora apertura*—Fig. 16f) has a round hole in the crown of its hat through which a fleshy tube protrudes making an exhalent current. During its life the mantle forms a fold over the front of the shell and hides the head. The slit limpet (*Emarginula reticulata*—Fig. 16g) has a very dark shell with strong radial ribs and a slit in the front margin. A tube

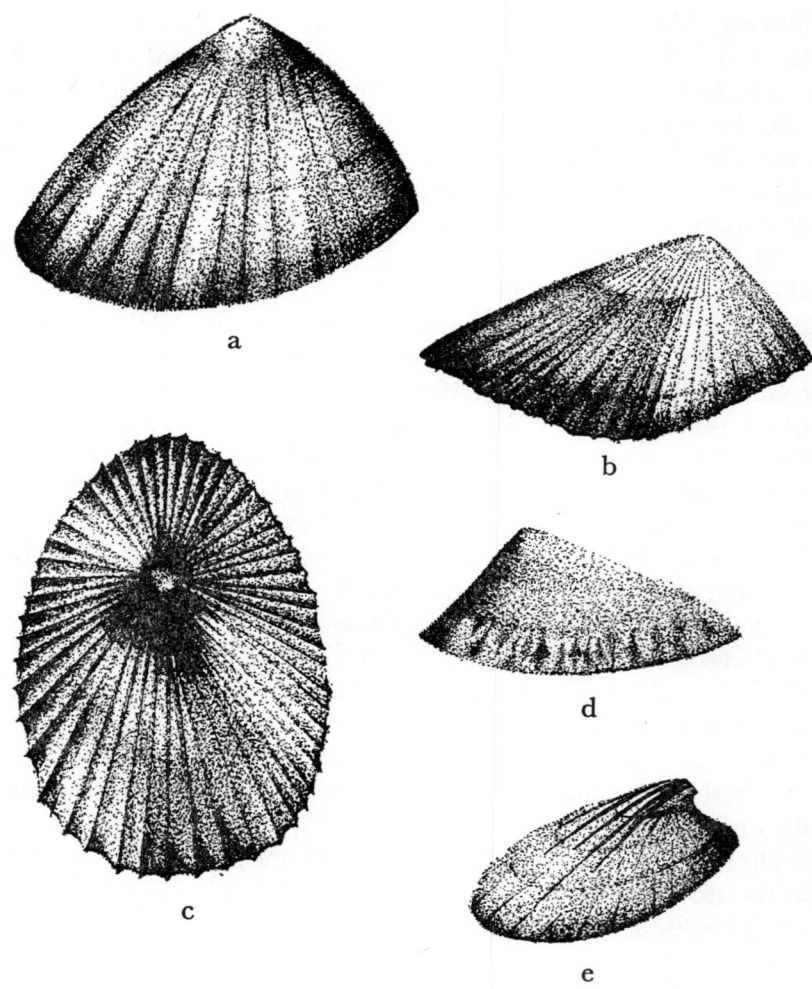

Fig. 16: Limpets

A. The Common Limpet: *Patella vulgata* × 1 nat. size. B. *Patella intermedia* × 2 nat. size approx. C. *Patella aspera* × 1¼ nat. size approx. D. The Tortoiseshell Limpet: *Acmaea tessulata* × 2 nat. size approx. E. The Blue-rayed Limpet: *Patina pellucida* × 2 nat. size approx.

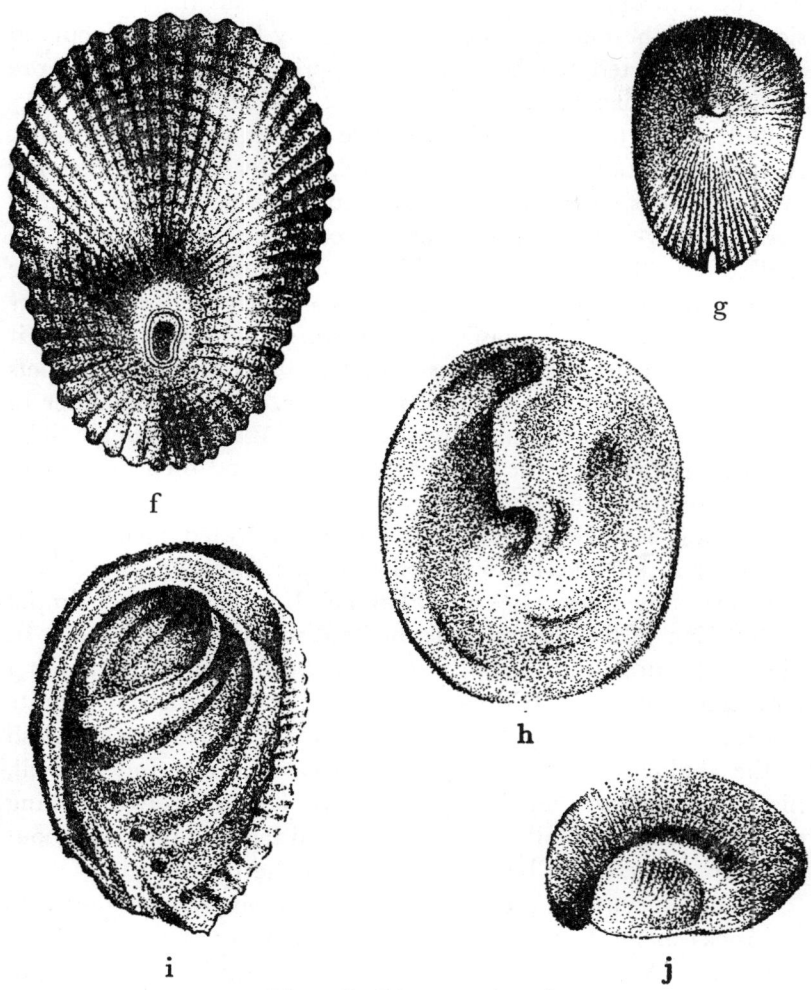

Fig. 16: Limpets (*cont.*)

F. The Keyhole Limpet: *Diodora apertura* × 2½ nat. size approx. G. The Slit Limpet: *Emarginula reticulata* × 2½ nat. size approx. H. The Chinaman's Hat: *Calyptraea chinensis* × 1¼ nat. size approx. I. The Ormer or Haliotis shell: *Haliotis tuberculata* × ½ nat. size approx. J. The Slipper Limpet: *Crepidula fornicata*, external view × ¾ nat. size approx.

protrudes through the upper part of this slit but there is no out-side fold of the mantle. The shell is slightly but distinctly curved and has deserted the hat shape, or perhaps it would be more true to say it has never achieved it.

Both these perforated limpets live low down on the shore. Another often found in the same zone, usually attached to stones or other shells, is the strangely shaped 'Chinaman's hat' (*Calyptraea chinensis*—Fig. 16h). It has a pronounced ledge within the shell and a columella in the middle, though the shell has from the outside the normal conical shape. It is a ciliary feeder and filters off fine particles of organic matter from the water current it creates by means of cilia on its gills. You often find these limpets in pairs or threes one on top of another. The first member to settle down is a male but subsequently changes to a female. The smaller males then settle down on top of her and then themselves later change sex and become females.

All these strange limpets with slit or perforated shells lead us to their relation, the haliotis shell or ormer (*Haliotis tuberculata*—Fig. 16i), sometimes called the 'abalone'. It is really a large limpet with a line of five perforations in its distinctly curved shell. In life a tube protrudes through each of the five openings making an exhalent current. It does not occur on our coasts but is quite common at low tide in the Channel Islands. In the East the flesh of the abalone is considered to be a great delicacy and its shell, highly polished so that the nacreous layer shows through, a thing of great beauty. While there may be different opinions about the former there can be no doubt about the latter.

When we come to the lamellibranchs or bivalves we find that the rocks themselves between the tide marks are not very richly populated. Most bivalves are burrowers living in sand or mud, a type of life for which they are specially adapted, and compara-tively few live on a hard substratum, clinging to rocks or stones by means of a fibrous beard or 'byssus'. Of these only the edible mussel is familiar to visitors to the shore on rocks between the tide marks. It grows in extraordinary profusion from below the lowest tides to about mid-shore, often in such dense masses that the shells are growing on each other. On sandy and muddy shores the

Plate 5.
Painted top
shells
(*Calliostoma
zizyphinum*)
with a single
grey top
(*Gibbula
cineraria*) at
the top of the
picture.
*Photo:
Douglas P.
Wilson, FRPS.*

Plate 6. Common dog whelks (*Nucella lapillus*) depositing egg capsules on the underside of a large stone which has been turned over in order to show them: a few young specimens are seen at left. *Photo: Douglas P. Wilson, FRPS.*

common mussel also grows in profusion wherever there are stones available to settle on and it is able to tolerate very brackish water, spreading far up estuaries almost into fresh water. The rapidity and ease with which mussels proliferate is illustrated by the fact that when the Dutch lowlands, flooded during the German invasion, were subsequently drained after the war, having been inundated by the sea for about a year, mussels were found to have formed colonies on the sides of houses, on fences and roadways, on telegraph poles, everywhere below flood level.

We have two edible mussels on our coasts, the common mussel (*Mytilus edulis*), which is found almost everywhere and reaches a length of about four inches, and the somewhat larger, stouter Mediterranean mussel (*M. galloprovincialis*—Pl. 9), which is found only on our south-western coasts and does not grow in estuaries. It reaches a length of about five inches and has a more downwardly curved beak than the common mussel.

Mussels breed by the simple method of spilling their eggs and sperm into the water. They are suspension feeders and entangle the plankton in the water current, wafted into the shell at the inhalent siphon, by means of strings of mucus on the gills. It is for this reason that they are able to live in such densely crowded colonies, for so long as they can draw in water there is never any lack of food for all.

The common mussel is equivalve, that is to say the two valves are the same size and shape, but markedly inequilateral. The part of the shell behind the beak or umbo, the normally central part of the hinge, the apex of the valve, is very much enlarged while the part in front is very much reduced. The beak, umbo or apex of the shell is thus at the extreme front end of the shell which is sharply pointed. The shape of the mussel is, as a result of this displacement, very well streamlined for living in positions where there is strong wave action. Its enlarged hinder end acts as a vane and ensures that the narrow beak points in the direction of flow of wave or tide. There are two adductor muscles but the anterior one is small and situated in the beak while the larger posterior one is in the wide rear part of the shell in front of the exhalent siphon.

5

We have several other marine mussels which live near or below
the level of the lowest tides. The horse mussel (*Modiolus modiolus*
Fig. 17a—see p. 99) lives below the lowest tides but its large
empty shells are sometimes found washed up on the beach after

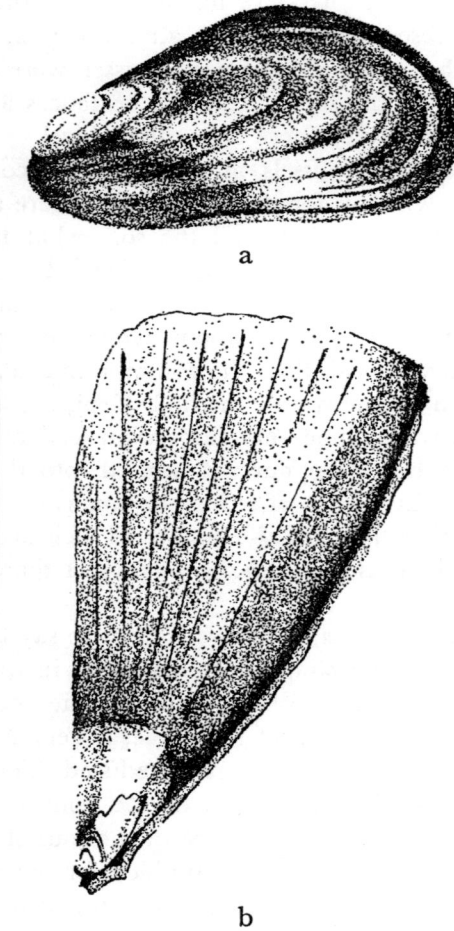

a

b

Fig. 17: Mussels

A. The Horse Mussel: *Modiolus modiolus* × ¾ nat. size approx.
B. The Fan Mussel: *Pinna fragilis* × ¾ nat. size approx.

rough weather. Four others live low down on the rocky shore, two permanently covered with a mat of fibres, the bearded horse mussel (*M. barbatus*) and the bean horse mussel (*M. phaseolinus*), and two small smooth ones with green shells, the marbled and the green crenella (*Musculus marmoratus* and *M. discors*). The bearded and bean horse mussels live on rocky ground or under rocks below low tide, the marbled crenella among Laminaria holdfasts and in the tests of sea-squirts, the green crenella among coralline seaweeds.

Since we are concerned with sea shells we shall not deal here with the fresh water mussels of which there are six species in Britain, two in ponds and lakes and four in rivers. They produce small larvae from inside a brood pouch and these pass through a parasitic stage on fish before they become adult mussels on the bed of the pond or river.

Low down on the rocks we shall find the common saddle oyster (*Anomia epihippum*—Fig. 27a). It is a small oyster belonging to a different family from that of the true oyster but nevertheless quite good to eat. It is very small, not much more than an inch across, and has a roughly circular, flat, whitish shell. Whereas the common oyster lives with the larger left valve below and the smaller right valve uppermost, the saddle oyster has the left valve uppermost. The lower right valve has a deep embayment, which later in life is completed to make a round hole below the apex of the shell. Through this embayment the threads of the byssus pass attaching the oyster to the rock face. The byssus calcifies as the embayment closes up so that the oyster becomes cemented to the rock by means of a solid calcareous pillar. As the saddle oyster grows the shape of the lower right valve follows the contours of the rock face so that the oyster comes to look like an encrusting growth. It is thus well adapted to withstand the battering of the waves on the exposed rock faces where it lives. Saddle oysters also occur encrusting on stones, the back of crabs and other shells.

A common bivalve of the rocky shore, though less familiar to the visitor than the mussel, clings in rock crevices by means of a very strong, tough, green byssus. This is the ark shell (*Arca tetragona*—Fig. 18a), the only common British representative of a family (Arcidae) which is numerous in warmer waters. It is found along the low tide mark, and thence down to about fifty fathoms, in crevices but also on stones and empty mollusc shells. It is about one and a half inches long and has a boat shape with the beaks of the two valves well forward and widely separated.

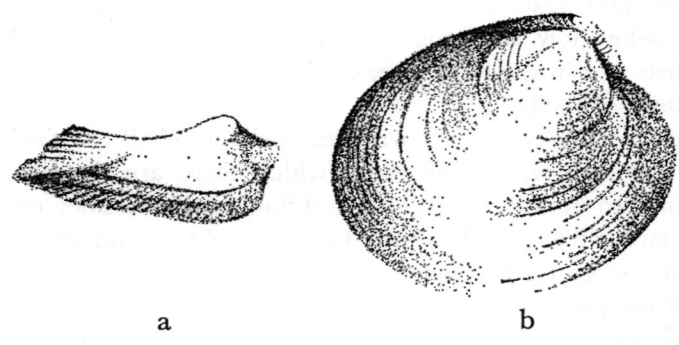

a   b

Fig. 18

A. The Ark shell: *Arca tetragona* × 1¼ nat. size. B. *Turtonia minuta* × 30 nat. size approx.

The hinge line between the two valves is quite straight with about 40 to 50 alternating small teeth and sockets (taxodont dentition), and the shell has radiating ridges.

Another common bivalve found almost anywhere between the tide marks is the tiny *Turtonia minuta*—(Fig. 18b). It is not more than one-sixteenth of an inch long, a plump, rounded shell, brown in colour but purplish around the umbo, fading to white near the margin. It is often found in dense masses clinging by its byssus in crevices. Again almost anywhere you look on the rocky shore you will notice tiny, oval, white bivalves (*Lasaea rubra*) clinging by means of a byssus to lichens or corallines, in empty barnacle cases and empty shells, in holdfasts of wracks and other weeds. They are less than one-twentieth of an inch in length and often clustered in enormous numbers, especially in cracks and crevices. They often share empty barnacle shells with the little banded snail, *Cingula*.

While most of our British bivalves are burrowers in sand or

mud, and so must be considered in another chapter, they can be found along the rocky shore in the sandy spits that fill the interstices among the rocks, or line the bottoms of pools, forming flat bays and coves among the rocks or grading gently into the shingle bank along the high tide mark. A number of others, which have a chapter to themselves, bore into the soft sandstone, limestone or chalk rocks excavating tunnels with their ridged shells.

Finally we must mention the coat-of-mail shells or chitons (Pl. 1) which, as already stated, belong to the primitive class Loricata. They are oval and shield-like with eight calcareous plates or scutes on their backs. In the tropics they run to a large size and may be four or five inches long, but our British ones are all small, half an inch or less. We have eight species but only one common one, *Lepidochitona cinereus*. It is red, brown, or green, with tufts of spines on either side of each plate. The chitons have the same rock-clinging habits as limpets and are found all over the shore on rocks or stones, usually in crevices. They can curl themselves around angularities of the rock and, when removed, will roll themselves almost but not quite into a ball like woodlice.

4

SPADEWORK ON THE SANDS

ALL we need now is a big iron spade. For on the sandy and muddy shore, where there is nothing to cling on to, not only molluscs but many other kinds of animals, worms, sea urchins, starfish and crustacea, have taken to a burrowing existence.

It is difficult to draw a very sharp distinction between the sandy, the gravelly and the muddy shore because to a certain extent the same shells are to be found in all three, but there are shells which may be most truly described as inhabitants of the sandy shore and those which may be truly looked upon as mud dwellers.

As one might expect the burrowing inhabitants of the shore are not sharply zoned from high to low tide. The fluctuations in the conditions of life, which are the primary cause of zoning on the rocks, do not affect the dark, wet, uniform world beneath the surface of the sand or mud. All that a burrowing animal need do when the tide goes out is to burrow deeper in order to maintain the amount of moisture it needs. For this reason most of the burrowing shells inhabit a zone from about mid-shore out to the shallow sublittoral. Few are found above mid-shore, more inhabit the low tide zone and more still the sublittoral zone which is never uncovered. Above mid-shore they would have to burrow too deep when the tide goes out. When collecting on a sandy or muddy shore, therefore, always dig as near low tide as possible. The population of burrowers is denser there and nearer to the surface, which saves digging.

Most of the burrowing shells are bivalves because they are the most perfectly adapted for this type of existence, not only by reason of their flattened shape but by reason also of their capacious gill chamber through which a current of water is perpetually drawn over the gills. Their method of suspension and deposit feeding also ensures that food will come to them automatically without their being obliged to go in search of it. A carnivorous

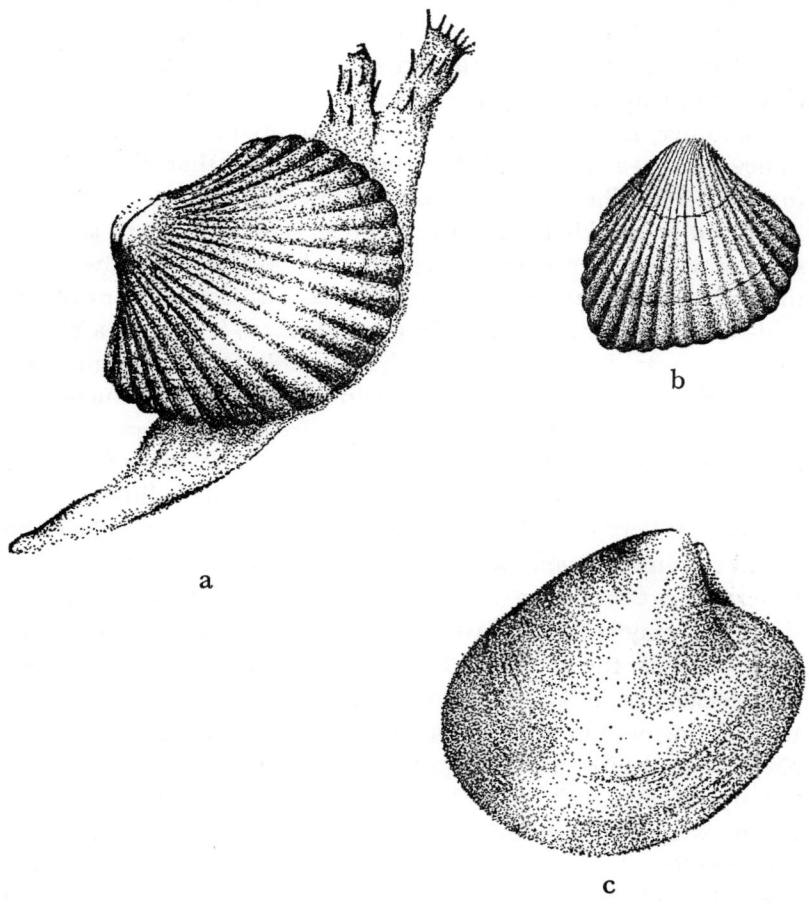

Fig. 19

A. The Common Cockle: *Cerastoderma (Cardium) edule* × 1½ nat. size approx. with inhalent (*right*) and exhalent (*left*) siphons extended.
B. The Little Cockle: *Pavicardium exiguum* × 1¾ nat. size approx.
C. The Iceland Cyprina: *Arctica islandica* × ½ nat. size approx.

or herbivorous feeding habit, involving hunting or browsing, would obviously be impossible for a burrowing mollusc.

The most familiar bivalves of the sandy shore are the cockles. The only one commonly found above the low tide mark is the edible cockle (*Cerastoderma* (*Cardium*) *edule*—Fig. 19a), a large, rather rounded shell with pronounced concentric ridges and radial ribs. It has prominent arched beaks well separated and facing one another, not turned forwards as in many other bivalves, but somewhat in advance of the middle line so that the shell is inequilateral. The colour is white, yellow, or brown.

The edible cockle likes to live in clean sand with clear, shallow swift-moving water flowing over it, and does not burrow more than about two inches below the surface. It occurs from about mid-shore to below low tide. In general, then, it lives in a rather shifting, unstable substratum so that its globular shape and pattern of ribs and ridges on the shell help to keep it firmly anchored. Some of the other cockles which live offshore have spines, processes and warts on their shells which assist this anchoring function, and are adaptations to a shifting habitat. The edible cockle, however, is very catholic in its choice of substratum and may be found in sand, gravelly sand, muddy sand and pure mud. But it generally prefers clean sand and, where it finds a favourable situation, may occur in vast numbers so as to form a hard platform of shells, the cockle bed, just below the surface of the sand. In a cockle bed in South Wales 462 million cockles were estimated to be living within an area of 320 acres (C. M. Yonge, *The Sea Shore*). Another estimate of population density is 10,000 cockles per square metre (N. Tebble, *British Bivalve Sea Shells*). Perhaps again owing to the shifting nature of the substratum cockles move about quite a lot, and sometimes the entire population of a cockle bed will suddenly upstakes and move off somewhere else in a mass.

The cockle can move by ploughing through the sand with its powerful foot, shaped like a ploughshare, but it can also jump by flexing and then quickly straightening the foot. This usually has the effect of making the shell roll over a few times, but it may give it a slight jump in the air if the kick from the foot is effective enough. There is no byssus or beard because the cockle has nothing to hang on to.

The cockle is a suspension feeder. The edges of the mantle around the inhalent and exhalent siphons are drawn out so as to form two separate tubes, a wide short inhalent and a narrower even shorter exhalent one. Both siphons are fringed with fleshy processes which are sensory. The two tubes thus act as a snorkel apparatus when the shell is below the surface of the sand, the inhalent tube drawing water into the mantle cavity, where the suspended plankton and organic matter is entangled in mucus on the gills, and the exhalent tube passing the water out.

The edible cockle is gathered commercially at several places around the British coasts, usually in estuaries since it tolerates very brackish water. There are cockle fisheries in the Wash, Thames estuary, Morecambe Bay, the Dee estuary, Dublin Bay, Carmarthen Bay and Burry Inlet, South Wales.

There are several other cockles around our coasts besides the edible one but they occur offshore below the low tide mark and are not likely to be found on shore, though their cast up shells may be (see. p. 106). Cockle shells are rather soft and their sculpturings are apt to get easily worn away which makes cast up shells very difficult to identify.

Another bivalve which, like the cockle, lies only just beneath the surface of the sand with its short siphon projecting above it is the Iceland cyprina (*Arctica islandica*—Fig. 19c). It is an almost completely round white or pale yellow shell, its white colour in life masked by a thick brown periostracum or horny layer which is usually worn off in cast up shells. It is one of the largest of our bivalves reaching a length of five inches. The valves are very inequilateral with curved beaks pointing forward and they are sculptured by many fine concentric ridges. The cyprina is really an offshore shell but it is also found on beaches at extreme low tide, and its cast up shells are quite common. Like the cockle it is very mobile and ploughs through the sand with its powerful foot.

We now come to three kinds of burrowing bivalves which can be found on any sandy, and sometimes on a muddy, shore, usually near the low tide mark. These are the venus clams, carpet shells and trough shells.

Venus shells (Veneridae) are marked by many concentric ridges and their beaks are turned towards the front end of the shell which is thus inequilateral, with the front margin a good deal shorter than the rear one.

Carpet shells belong to the same family but have a rather more rounded, less prominent beak than the venus shells. The beak is

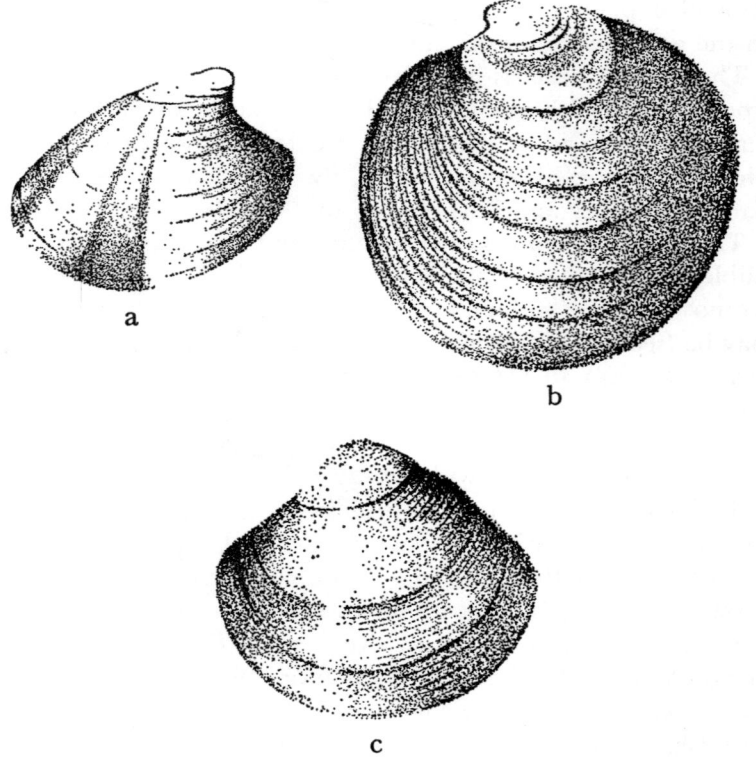

Fig. 20: Venus shells

A. The Striped Venus: *Venus striatula* × 1½ nat. size. B. The Rayed Artemis shell: *Dosinia exoleta* × 4 nat. size approx. C. The American Quahog or Hard-shell Clam: *Venus mercenaria* × 1 nat. size approx.

less turned towards the front but is situated farther forward than that of venus shells so that the outline of the carpet shell is more asymmetrical.

Trough shells (Mactridae) have a symmetrical, triangular

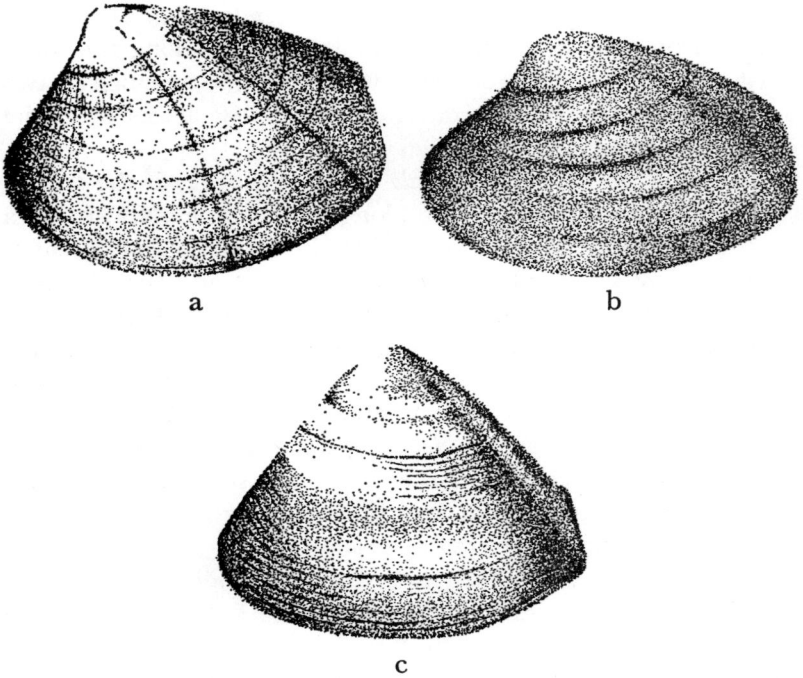

a   b

c

Fig. 21 : Carpet and Trough shells

A. The Cross-cut Carpet shell: *Venerupis decussata* × ¾ nat. size. B. The Pullet Carpet shell: *Venerupis pallustra* × ¾ nat. size. C. The Thick Trough shell: *Spisula solida* × 2 nat. size approx.

shape with rounded angles, the shell being equivalve and equila- teral. The valves are smooth or only slightly ridged.

There are several venus shells which are common on sandy shores, the striped venus (*Venus striatula*—Fig. 20a) with three brown rays on a yellow ground; the oval venus (*V. ovata*), smaller and pinkish with 40 to 50 radiating ribs; the banded venus

(*V. fasciata*), on and below the middle shore, yellow, pink, red, and brown with darker rays; and the rayed artemis shell (*Dosinia exoleta*—Fig. 20b) which is quite round in outline, about two inches in diameter and has many finely chiselled, prominent, concentric ridges—a beautiful shell, pale yellow in colour.

The cross-cut carpet shell (*Venerupis decussata*—Fig. 21a), often common on sand or muddy gravel at low tide along the south coast, is a fine heavily-built shell which may be as much as two inches long. It has many concentric ridges cut across by radial ribs, hence the name.

The thick trough shell (*Spisula solida*—Fig. 21c) is the trough shell you are most likely to find along the low tide mark. It has a very solid triangular shell, pale yellow in colour, with concentric smooth grooves rather than ridges. About one and three-quarter inches long the valves are more nearly equilateral than those of any other trough shell. The most abundant and famous of the trough shells is the cut trough shell (*S. subtruncata*) which lives in enormous abundance in shallow waters offshore (see p. 106).

The rayed trough shell (*Mactra corallina*) is common on clean sand at very low tide and offshore. It has a smooth brittle shell, not thick and coarse like the thick and cut troughs, and has brown radiating rays on a white creamy ground.

The glaucous trough shell (*M. glauca*) is similar to the rayed trough but has paler rays. It is one of the largest bivalves on our coasts and may reach a length of three and three-quarter inches, whereas the other members of this group seldom reach one and three-quarter inches. The glaucous trough is rare but can occasionally be dug up at extreme low springs in Cornwall. It is creamy white in colour with pale brown radiating rays.

All these shells are suspension feeders. They live just beneath the surface of the sand drawing water into their shells and wafting it out again through short joined or separated siphons. Their food is essentially plankton and organic refuse.

There is, however, a family of bivalves which live just below the surface of the sand but are deposit feeders, relying for their nourishment not on the plankton suspended in the inhalent current but on the fine deposit of organic detritus or rubbish on the surface of the sand and it is this which they suck in with the inhalent current. Their siphons are separate and are longer than those of the suspension feeders, though not as long as those of the deep burrowing bivalves to be mentioned later (pp. 87–89). These are the wedge shells (Donacidae) of which the best known is the purple-toothed or banded wedge shell (*Donax vittatus*—Fig. 22a). The wedge shells are, as their name implies, wedge-shaped, broader but much flatter and thinner than venus, carpet or trough shells, with the beak well forward so that the valves are very inequilateral and their shape is that of a rectangle with rounded corners. They are thick, highly polished, smooth shells without ribs or ridges. The banded wedge is one of the loveliest shells on our beaches. Its smooth flat valves may be white, yellow, brown, or purple, with several concentric bands of deeper colour. There are often three rays of white radiating from the beak and many very fine radiating lines which fade out before they reach the margin of the shell. The margins of the valves are purple inside no matter what the outside colour may be and are serrated with many very fine teeth.

The banded wedge lives only just under the surface of the sand near the low water mark and, where it finds suitable conditions, it is often very abundant. It is a highly mobile shell and can move about over the sand with ease, helped very greatly by its thin flat shape. This mobility, one may assume, is an adaptation to its feeding habit since, in spite of being a deposit feeder, it likes clean sandy exposed shores where the supply of organic detritus must be rather scarce.

There are a number of bivalves, most of them inhabiting both sand and mud, which burrow deeply and may, indeed, go down a foot or more. Most of them have very long snorkel tubes which enable them to do this, though the razor shells, as we shall see (p. 81), have adopted another device.

The tellins (Tellinidae) are flattened rounded shells with a large elastic ligament externally between the valves. When you find empty tellin shells they are always wide open with the valves gaping owing to the strong action of this ligament. The shell is so very flattened that it is difficult to believe that a body with all

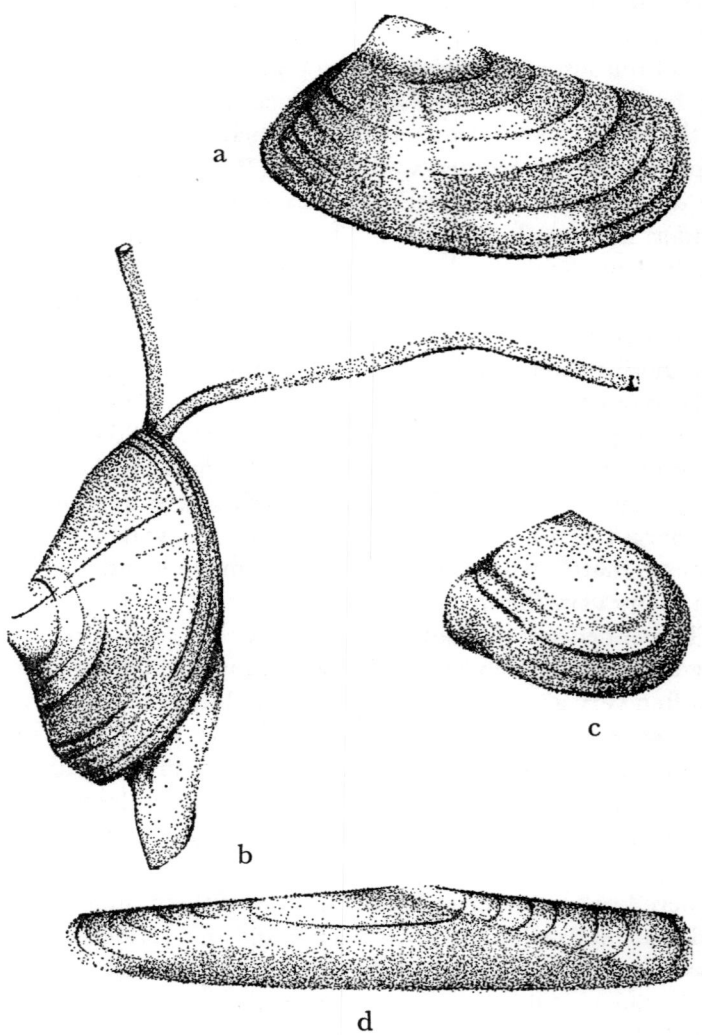

Fig. 22: Wedge shells and Tellins

A. The Purple Toothed or Banded Wedge shell: *Donax vittatus* $\times$ $1\frac{1}{2}$ nat. size approx. B. The Thin Tellin: *Tellina tenuis* $\times$ 2 nat. size. C. The Baltic Tellin: *Macoma balthica* $\times$ $1\frac{1}{2}$ nat. size approx. D. *Pharus legumen* $\times$ 2 nat. size approx.

its organs can be contained within the smooth, delicate, translucent valves. The foot is very long and thin, seeming to exude from between the valves almost like a liquid, and the tellin can move through the sand by means of it very rapidly. The tellins are deposit feeders with the separate inhalent and exhalent siphons very long fine tubes several times the length of the shell when extended. The inhalent siphon is about twice the length of the exhalent one and lies on the surface of the sand searching about like the tube of a vacuum cleaner sucking up the layer of fine deposit.

As you approach the extreme edge of the water on a beach of clean sand you may see small bivalves disappearing beneath the moist surface before your advancing footsteps. These will be either wedge shells (*Donax*—above) or they may be our commonest tellin, the thin tellin (*Tellina tenuis*—Fig. 22b). It is pink or white with a very flattened shape and about three-quarters of an inch in length. It occurs, sometimes in enormous numbers, from the edge of extreme low tide up to about mid-shore. Several other tellins live offshore while others live in muddy estuaries and will be mentioned later (p. 88).

Perhaps the most familiar of the burrowing bivalves are the razor shells whose widely gaping, elongated, pod-shaped valves, black outside and pearly within, are common enough on sandy and muddy beaches cast up along the high tide mark. We have in the first place to distinguish between one species of razor shell, whose hinge and ligament between the elongated valves are centrally placed, and the others whose hinge and ligament are situated right at the front end, that is, at the bottom of the tube formed by the valves when the shell is upright in its burrow. The first (*Pharus legumen*—Fig. 22d) is really closely related to the tellins and has long separate siphons emerging from the upper end of the tube. It lives in clean sand from low down on the beach to some way offshore and moves so swiftly in a vertical direction in the sand that it is very difficult to bring up a specimen intact.

This ability to pull themselves down vertically with great rapidity is a characteristic which all the razor shells have in common. A powerful, immensely elongated, tapering foot thrusts

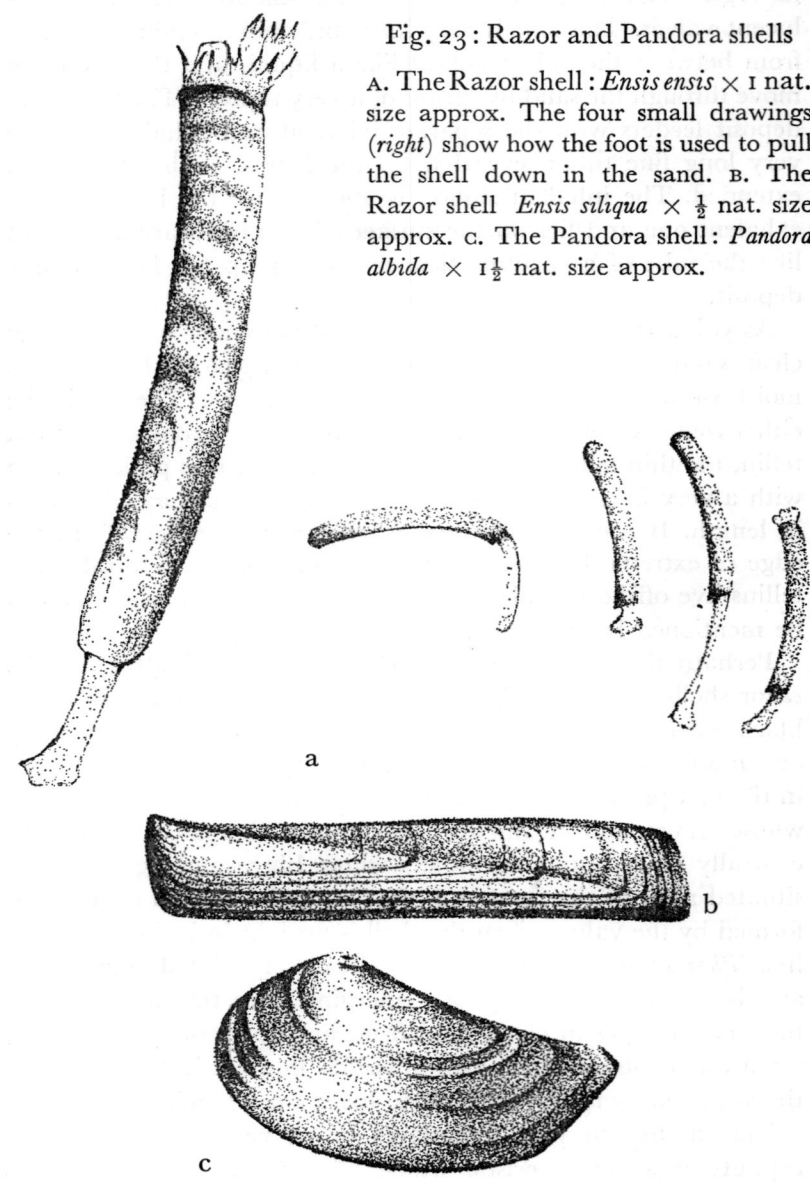

Fig. 23 : Razor and Pandora shells

A. The Razor shell : *Ensis ensis* × 1 nat. size approx. The four small drawings (*right*) show how the foot is used to pull the shell down in the sand. B. The Razor shell *Ensis siliqua* × ½ nat. size approx. C. The Pandora shell : *Pandora albida* × 1½ nat. size approx.

a

b

c

Plate 7. A common dog whelk (band?d variety) boring into a mussel: the hole made by a previous attempt in the thicker part of the mussel's shell can be seen. *Photo: Douglas P. Wilson, FRPS.*

Plate 8. Cowries (*Trivia monacha*) at the base of a
'knobbly sea-squirt' (*Phallusia mamillata*). *Photo:
Douglas P. Wilson, FRPS.*

out at the front (bottom) end of the tube formed by the two valves. Normally, when sitting in its burrow covered by the tide, the razor shell is quite near the surface (Fig. 23a). All the true razors (not *Pharus* which is really a tellin) have two quite short siphons which project slightly above the surface of the substratum. When the tide recedes the razor shell pulls itself down vertically. Each one betrays its presence by a small crater in the sand marking its position. As the animal retreats farther at your approach a little spurt of water and sand is shot up in the middle of the crater. The animal pulls itself down by thrusting its tapering foot vertically downwards. It then swells out the tip of the foot by engorging it with blood so as to make it into a sort of anchor. It then pulls down upon this mushroom-shaped expansion by means of strong muscles in the foot. At the end of each downward thrust the valves gape apart slightly inside the burrow so as to hold the shell in position while the foot, now deflated and tapering again, makes another downward probe. Then, when the foot expands and the muscles pull the shell down once more, the valves close and enable the shell to slide downwards. If the valves did not open between thrusts the shell would be forced upwards when the foot pushed downwards into the sand. Thus, by means of a series of swift, powerful thrusts and pulls the razor shell can move downwards in the sand with astonishing speed. You have to be an expert with the spade and dig swiftly if you want to get a razor shell back whole. This spadework may be avoided by putting some salt on the crater which marks the razor shell's position. As this dissolves the locally increased salinity irritates the animal and causes it to protrude the hinder end of its shell from its burrow. With a swift, strong pull you may then perhaps be able to drag the animal out, but you must act quickly for if you give it time to pull down with its foot you will either lose it and see it vanish into the sand or you will be left with only a fragment of it.

The razor shells may have either straight or curved valves about eight times as long as they are broad, making a tube when apposed. We have two curved razors and two straight ones. The curved ones are *Ensis arcuata*, four inches long, and *E. ensis* (Fig. 23a) six inches long; both are common on the lower parts of clean

6

sandy beaches. One of the straight ones (*E. siliqua*—Fig. 23b), called the pod razor, is much longer, up to eight inches, with a square truncated front end. Another straight one, the grooved razor (*Solen marginatus*), prefers a muddy habitat and may burrow to a depth of eighteen inches. Another one, much smaller, only an inch in length (*Phaxas pellucidus*) lives offshore.

Before we leave the bivalves of the sandy shore we should mention the pandora shell (*Pandora albida*—Fig. 23c) which usually lives offshore on sand or muddy sand but does sometimes occur in considerable abundance along the low tide mark. It is very localized in its distribution, preferring very sheltered bays, and along our south coast especially favours the neighbourhood of Swanage. It also occurs along the western coasts of the British Isles and off the Channel Islands. The shell, about one and a half inches long, and whitish tinged with yellow, is markedly inequilateral and inequivalve. The posterior end of the shell is slightly upturned so as to form a sort of secondary apex. The left valve is curved and spoon-shaped while the right valve is flat and lies within the concavity of the left. The pandora is not a burrower but lies on the surface of the sand and has a very short siphon.

We might end this account of the burrowing bivalves of the sandy shore by including what the Americans call 'clams' but we call 'gapers' because the two hinder margins of the valves gape in order to accommodate the relatively enormous muscular siphons. But although these big shells are sometimes found on sandy beaches they greatly prefer mud and have many relations which are true denizens of the muddy shore, so I shall leave them until the next chapter.

When we come to the gastropods we find that there are as few true denizens of the sandy shore as there are bivalves which are true denizens of the rocky shore.

The netted dog whelk (*Nassarius reticulatus*—Fig. 14b) is a common inhabitant of the sand along the low tide mark and just offshore. It ploughs along at the surface, usually half buried with its long siphon tube projecting upwards. The shell is a rather high, thin spiral, one and a quarter inches in height, with a deep siphon groove in the margin of the aperture. It is marked by spiral ridges and vertical ribs which break the surface up into a network pattern, hence the name.

Besides this there are only two kinds of burrowing gastropods on the sandy shore. One is a family of carnivorous snails, the necklace shells (Naticidae), and the other comprises a few species of sea slugs (opisthobranch gastropods).

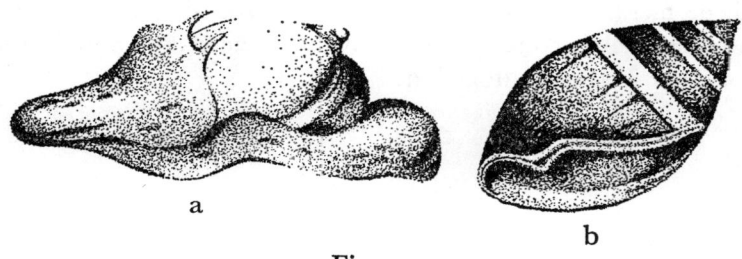

a   b

Fig. 24

A. The Common Necklace shell: *Natica alderi* × $1\frac{3}{4}$ nat. size approx. showing the appearance in life with the shell almost hidden by the reflected mantle. B. The Actaeon shell: *Actaeon tornatilis* × 2 nat. size.

The necklace shells are coiled, rounded snails with a large umbilicus and an ear-shaped operculum. They have an immensely large splayed-out foot which envelops a good deal of the shell and enables it to glide about over the surface of the soft sand as though on a snow-shoe. They are carnivorous and prey on burrowing bivalves, boring into their shells with their radulae. The common necklace shell (*Natica alderi*—Fig. 24a) is pale brown or yellow, about three-quarters of an inch in height, and the large necklace shell (*N. catena*) is about twice that size, yellow with red vertical markings.

Like the necklace shells the sea slugs also have the shell to a greater or lesser extent enveloped in the mantle. In the beautiful actaeon shell (*Actaeon tornatilis*—Fig. 24b) the animal can be completely withdrawn into the elongated aperture of its shell so that it looks like a true snail, though very much elongated and pointed. When the animal is extruded the flesh of the mantle covers the shell and head while the broad flattened tentacles are carried erect. Like that of the necklace shell this expanded mantle enables the actaeon to glide about over the surface of the sand as well as burrowing. The actaeon is found low down on sandy beaches and is one of the most beautiful of our shells with an elongated, conical spire, red in colour, banded with white spirals.

Two other sea slugs, the bubble shells, also occasionally occur in sand but they are really inhabitants of the muddy shore and will be mentioned later (p. 91). Among sea slugs generally we find the shell becoming progressively reduced and fragile until in some it is absent altogether.

5

SPADEWORK IN THE MUD

M U D is, generally speaking, a more satisfactory medium for burrowing animals, especially molluscs, than sand. It settles gently in calm water and forms a compact and stable mass. It does not get constantly swirled about and shifted by tides, currents and waves as sand is apt to. Burrowing bivalves, therefore, do not have to be mobile in mud as they do in sand, ready as it were to move off at a moment's notice when the world collapses around them. Nor do they need to have projections, ribs or ridges to help them to anchor themselves in their substratum. In mud, therefore, shells tend to have smooth, globular outlines. But one of the hazards of life in mud arises from increasing lateral pressure or change of pressure as the mud deposit accumulates and packs down. For this reason burrowing bivalves in mud tend to have thickly built robust shells. Further, for deposit feeders mud is an excellent medium because in estuaries, where mud flats mainly occur, there is always a dense layer of organic matter brought down by the river, settling gently but continually on the mud surface.

In any typical estuary we pass gradually from a shore of sand and muddy sand, or of gravelly sand, where the water is saline, through coarse mud and finally to fine impalpable mud. The water becomes more and more brackish and when the salinity falls to a certain point the fine mud precipitates and packs down on the bottom.

In estuarine shores of muddy sand we may look for the clams or gapers. The commonest is the American soft-shelled clam or, as we call it, the sand gaper (*Mya arenaria*—Fig. 25a). On the eastern coast of the United States it occurs in enormous numbers and is often protected by law because it is a commercial article

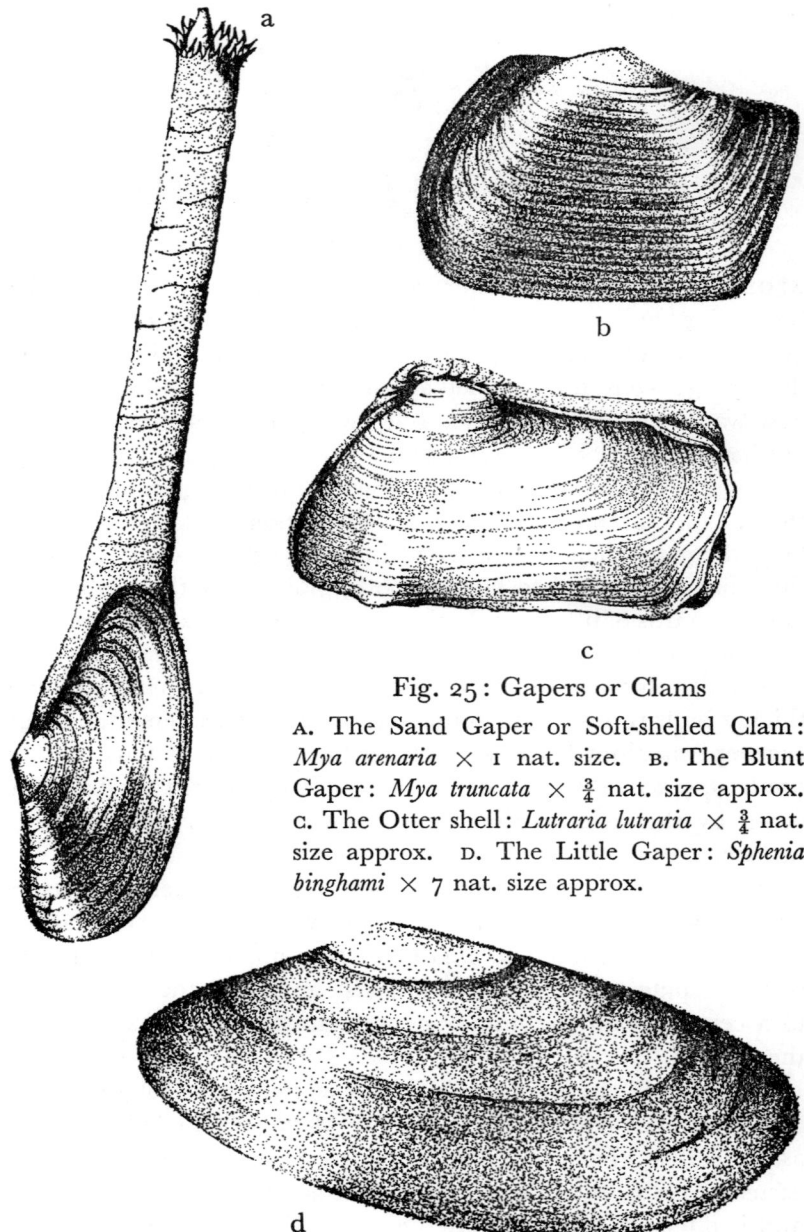

Fig. 25 : Gapers or Clams

A. The Sand Gaper or Soft-shelled Clam:
Mya arenaria × 1 nat. size. B. The Blunt
Gaper: *Mya truncata* × $\frac{3}{4}$ nat. size approx.
C. The Otter shell: *Lutraria lutraria* × $\frac{3}{4}$ nat.
size approx. D. The Little Gaper: *Sphenia
binghami* × 7 nat. size approx.

of food. The 'clam bake' in the States is a great pastime for young and old. In our estuaries the clam is common enough too and I have dug for them in Salcombe Bay, Devon.

The common clam or sand gaper is a big, heavy, oval, dull-looking shell, dirty white or fawn coloured, with a thick outer horny layer or periostracum which is continued on to the enormous double trunk of the siphon, about two and a half times the length of the shell itself. The hinder margins of the valves gape apart so as to accommodate this immense trunk, hence the name 'gaper'. A characteristic feature of the articulation of the two valves is the large spoon-shaped projection, called the 'chondrophore' (literally, the 'cartilage bearer') which projects inwards beneath the beak of the left valve in order to carry the attachment of the strong internal ligament.

When the clam is young the shell is rounder than that of the adult and the conjoined inhalent and exhalent siphons are comparatively short. The foot is large and the animal moves about over the surface of the sand, perhaps attaching itself temporarily to stones or shells by means of a long slender byssus thread. But eventually the clam takes to burrowing vertically just below the surface with its foot. Once settled in a satisfactory position it does not move again unless disturbed. As it grows older the clam slowly descends deeper, the foot growing smaller until it is less than half the length of the shell. The foot remains functionless unless and until the animal is compelled for any reason to make another burrow for itself. The byssus thread disappears. As the shell descends deeper in the sand the siphons enlarge and extend, keeping the two openings, fringed with tentacles, at the surface.

The common clam is one of the largest of our bivalves and may reach a length of five inches. The siphon trunk is then at least a foot long. The blunt gaper (*M. truncata*—Fig. 25b), which is almost as common as the sand gaper or clam, is considerably smaller and is immediately identifiable by the square truncated rear end of its shell. It lives in stiff compact mud.

The otter shells (Lutrariidae) have a manner of life similar to the gapers and their valves, too, gape widely to accommodate the large siphon tube. They are, however, more closely related to the trough shells than to the clams, are more oval in shape than the true gapers and do not have the large spoon-shaped chondrophore in the left valve. Instead they have a triangular pit beneath the beak in both valves. They are olive brown in colour, though the shell beneath the periostracum is fawn or white. The tissue of the siphon tube is transparent and pale in colour while that of the true gapers is opaque and dark. The otter shells are also among the largest British bivalves and the common otter (*Lutraria lutraria*—Fig. 25c) reaches a length of five inches. It lives mainly in muddy sand but also in sand and gravel. Offshore we have two other otters which live in shelly and muddy gravel.

The burrowing bivalves typical of the sandy shore are also found in estuarine regions of muddy sand, but as we go upstream towards the finer mud and more brackish water these shells gradually fade out and are replaced by truly mud-dwelling shells.

The cockle is found in muddy sand but is less abundant than in clean sand and in fine mud is replaced by the little cockle (*Pavicardium exiguum*—Fig. 19b) which is only about half an inch long and has warts or tubercles on the ribs, on all of them when young but only on the anterior ones in older shells. The little cockle is found very low on the mud flat near the low tide mark. The thin tellin (*Tellina tenuis*) of the sandy shore is replaced in mud by the Baltic tellin (*Macoma balthica*—Fig. 22c) which is rounder and stouter and does not move about so much, but occurs in brackish estuaries in enormous numbers.

The cross-cut carpet shell (*Venerupis decussata*), already mentioned as common on sand, also occurs in muddy sand where it is joined by another carpet shell, the pullet carpet shell (*V. pullastra*—Fig. 21b). This is a big shell, up to two inches long, cream, yellowish, or grey, with brown mottlings around the margin supposed, in a somewhat far-fetched analogy, to resemble those on the plumage of some young pullets—hence the name. It is usually found in muddy sand around the bases of rocks or big stones often attached by a byssus.

In true mud these two shells are replaced by their mud dwelling counterpart, the hard-shell clam or American quahog (*Venus mercenaria*—Fig. 20c). This is a solid, dirty white, oval shell about two inches long marked by concentric lines. Like all venus shells it is inequilateral with the beaks placed forward and curling over. It is properly a native of the eastern coast of the United States where it is extremely popular as food, but it has been introduced into British waters. It was first found here in the middle of the last century in the Mersey and Humber estuaries but is now abundant in the Solent, Southampton Water and Portsmouth Harbour where it is presumed to have started colonies as a result of being thrown overboard from liners.

As we move (with difficulty and probably sheathed in magnificent black mud to far above the knees) up the estuary into the regions of fine mud we shall find that all the other shells are being replaced by the true mud dwellers, the furrow shells (Scrobiculariidae), of which the commonest is the peppery furrow shell (*Scrobicularia plana*—Fig. 26a). This is an oval, almost though not quite symmetrical equilateral shell, grey, light brown, or yellow in colour, about two and a half inches long and flat, rather like a tellin. It has a large foot for burrowing but is not in fact very mobile. It has two very long separated siphons, the inhalent more than twice the length of the exhalent. In large specimens the inhalent siphon may be as much as six inches long. As the shell lies buried just below the surface of the mud the inhalent siphon searches about over it sucking in the deposit of organic detritus with such force that after a while a groove appears in the mud wherever it has been operating. The siphons are, of course, withdrawn when the tide goes out but the position of the shell is always marked by furrows, arranged in a star pattern, caused by the vigorous sucking action of the inhalent siphon operating when the tide covers it. It is from these patterns that the shell gets its name.

A relation of the furrow shell is *Abra*, a genus of which there are two principal species in our waters, *A. tenuis* and *A. alba*, the thin and the white furrow shells. They usually occur in southern estuaries and are small, fairly symmetrical dirty white shells.

The little oval bivalve, *Lasaea rubra*, which we found clinging to lichens and corallines and in the cases of barnacles along the rocky shore, has its muddy counterpart in a somewhat fatter, rounder shell, *Kellia suborbicularis*, which also lives in dead shells and in cracks and crevices.

As in sand so in mud gastropods are comparatively few but

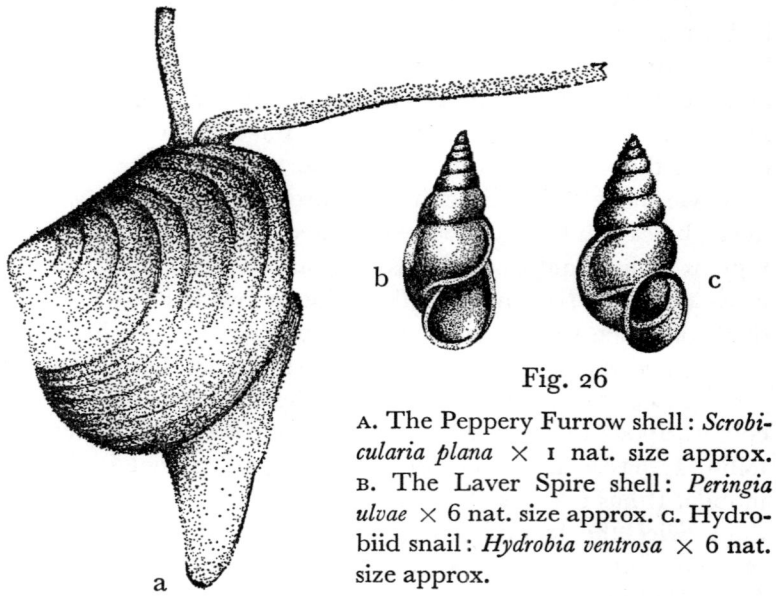

Fig. 26

A. The Peppery Furrow shell: *Scrobicularia plana* × 1 nat. size approx. B. The Laver Spire shell: *Peringia ulvae* × 6 nat. size approx. C. Hydrobiid snail: *Hydrobia ventrosa* × 6 nat. size approx.

there are several tiny spire shells, the Hydrobiid snails, which often occur over the muddy shore in enormous numbers. One is the laver spire shell (*Peringia ulvae*—Fig. 26b), a tiny, pointed, dark coloured snail which sometimes covers the surface of estuarine mud in such numbers as to give it the appearance of caviar. It is specially abundant where the filmy green sea lettuce (*Ulva lactuca*) grows and is often found plentifully far from the sea in the dykes and ditches of salt marshes. When the water covers the mud these tiny snails burrow beneath the surface but come out into the air again when the tide recedes. A slightly larger, thicker cousin, Jenkins' spire shell (*Potamopyrgus jenkinsi*), lives far up the estuaries in almost completely fresh water and a third (*Hydrobia ventrosa*—Fig. 26c) is found in all brackish estuaries, especially on our south and east coasts.

Two bubble shells (sea slugs—opisthobranch gastropods) are denizens of the muddy shore. One, *Haminoea navicula,* has a very fragile coiled shell completely enveloped in the mantle, and a large foot with two lateral wings which are used for swimming. The other bubble shell (*Haminoea hydatis*) has an oblong, more solid coiled shell with an elongated aperture, but the animal cannot withdraw into it. A third one, the soft bubble shell (*Akera bullata*—Pl. 10) is rather rare but may be found on beds of eel grass (*Zostera marina*), the only true flowering plant that grows in the sea. In England eel grass became almost extinct at one time but is now recovering. The soft bubble shell is glossy green and semi-transparent and has a long filament projecting from the spire. The body is grey, white, or orange speckled with dark colours. In the spring breeding season it swims actively about by means of the wing-like extensions of the foot, but at all other times it sits on the bottom with its wings wrapped around it.

6

BELOW LOW TIDE

WITH a face mask and breathing tube we can take a look at the seaward faces of the rocks below the lowest springs, the truly sub-littoral rocky zone among the thong weeds and strap weeds which are never really uncovered. It is important to choose a calm day for this because rocks covered with profuse growths of large barnacles, mussels and rock oysters are dangerous if there is a strong tide or heavy swell. A sudden surge against these surfaces can result in painful abrasions or even broken limbs.

We shall find a number of shells fixed to the rocks by means of a byssus and others crawling about or hiding in crevices. Several kinds of large and beautiful shells are more likely to be found on bottoms of sand or gravel, in the interstices of the rocks or in deep creeks and chasms with sand or gravel or small stones at the bottom of them.

Several splendid large snails belonging to the whelk family live in this sort of location. The best known and most familiar is the common whelk or buckie (*Buccinum undatum*). Small specimens of this fine shell are sometimes found between the tide marks low down on the shore and we often see large empty specimens on the beach which have been taken over by hermit crabs. But large living specimens are not often seen above the low tide mark. The buckie is a stoutly built, yellowish white snail, the largest coiled shell on our coasts, reaching a length of six inches on offshore bottoms. It has seven or eight whorls with pronounced spiral ridges and the oval aperture has a long spout-like siphonal canal. Like all the whelks the buckie is a carnivorous snail and ploughs about over the sand and rocks with its powerful foot, its siphon tube upraised like a periscope. With its efficient radula it drills holes in the shells of bivalves and other gastropods.

Another whelk is the spindle shell (*Neptunea antiqua*—Fig. 14c). Its empty shells, too, are often found cast up on the beach or occupied by hermit crabs but live shells are seldom found on the shore. It really lives below the low tide mark where large specimens rival the buckie in size. The white shell is smooth but the whorls are marked by a single pronounced spiral ridge. The rather narrow oval aperture has a very long siphonal spout or canal which gives an almost fusiform shape to the shell.

Both buckie and spindle shells when found on the beach, especially if inhabited by hermit crabs, are often covered by a furry-looking pelt which, on close inspection, can be seen to consist of a mass of tiny hydroids (*Hydractinia echinata*) which live on the shell in association with the hemit crab.

The buckie deposits large round egg masses among the rocks. After the young have crawled out of the capsules the whole mass becomes detached and drifts away. After a spell of rough weather you can see these masses of egg capsules cast up on the shore along the high tide mark looking like dried sponges.

The common, netted and thick-lipped dog whelks found on rocks between the tide marks are also to be seen in the sublittoral zone but there are two other whelks, rather smaller, about two inches long, which are pests of oyster beds but are nevertheless often found far removed from oysters at extreme low tide and below on stony ground, rocks, sand or muddy sand, preying on bivalves and barnacles. They, like other whelks, bore into their prey through the shell and rasp out the living contents with their radulae. One of these is the sting winkle (*Ocenebra erinacea*—Pl. 12) which has a whitish rough shell, very much ridged. In old shells the aperture is quite round, the siphonal canal, which was visible in the young shell, having closed up. The sting winkle, although really an offshore snail, moves up the beach in the spring in order to lay its flask-shaped egg capsules. It is really a warm water shell and is almost exterminated around our coasts whenever we have a cold winter, only to recover when the spring comes. It really prefers oysters and drills into the upper valve, rasping out the oyster inside. Nowadays, however, it has spread far beyond the oyster beds. It was originally named *Murex* and, like other members of that genus, it carries behind its head a sack of dye which turns purple when exposed to the air.

The other whelk, also a pest of oysters, is an unwelcome visitor from America and was brought over in about 1880 when attempts were being made to replenish our dwindling oyster beds with American blue point oysters (see pp. 98–99). Unfortunately the American oyster pests were brought over as well as the oysters. The American oysters failed because they could not breed in our cold waters, but the pests succeeded beyond expectations; they remained and bred, spreading all along the coast far beyond the oyster beds. One of these imported pests is the American oyster drill (*Urosalpinx cinerea*—Fig. 14d), a brownish shell, rather smaller than the sting winkle with more pronounced vertical ribs and a well-marked siphonal canal that does not close up in later life. Its habits are very much like those of the sting winkle but it is hardier and can withstand cold winters.

Another oyster pest, brought over from America at the same time as the oyster drill, is the slipper limpet (*Crepidula fornicata*—Fig. 16j), which has now spread all around our shores and to the northern coast of Europe, living in abundance on rocky shores below the low water line. It is a strange-looking shell, not really very closely related to the true limpet, with a shelf half way across the base so that when viewed from underneath it looks rather like a slipper. The umbo or apex of the conical brown shell is turned over like a liberty cap. Like the Chinaman's hat (p. 64) the slipper limpet lives in groups or chains of up to a dozen animals piled on top of one another. The lowest in the pile are the oldest and are always females. The youngest are males and those in between are intermediate, changing from male to female. A sex change takes place from male to female in the life of each shell. Slipper limpets grow in such profusion on oyster beds that, without directly damaging the oysters, they simply smother them. The slipper limpet is a ciliary suspension feeder and forms such masses on top of the oysters that the suspended plankton is filtered off from the water before the oysters get a chance so that they die of starvation and suffocation.

Smaller and less abundant than the slipper limpet is the bonnet limpet (*Capulus ungaricus*—Pl. 11) which forms smaller chains with the female underneath and several males above on oysters and scallops.

Oysters themselves live on rocks or stones, shells or clean sand, below low tide mark under clear, clean shallow water, and are never uncovered. In chapter three we found saddle oysters clinging to the rocks along the low tide mark. In the last century the native oyster (*Ostrea edulis*—Fig. 27b) used to grow wild in abundance in suitable places around our southern coasts and was even taken in trawls in the North Sea, but nowadays, owing to pollution and the silting up of inshore breeding places, and to the depredations of oyster gatherers and the natural pests, oysters are mostly grown artificaly. Some are imported from France, where the greatest oyster breeding beds in the world are situated on the west coast near Arcachon, and fattened in special ponds near Colchester until they are four or five years old. Our own native oysters are bred and reared at the principal oyster beds which are also near Colchester.

The native oyster changes sex several times during a breeding season, being first female, then male and then, perhaps, female again. The actual number of changes seems to depend on the temperature of the water for in the French beds the oysters change sex two or three times in a season whereas in Denmark and in our beds they usually change only once. The Portuguese oyster does not change at all and the different shells are either male or female. In the spring and early summer months, May, June, July, August, when there is no 'r' in the month, the oysters produce enormous numbers of microscopic free-swimming bivalve larvae, called 'spat'. Each one swims by means of a crown of fine protoplasmic processes, or cilia; in fact, they do not really swim so much as drift about on the tide in clouds, for they are very tiny and helpless. Those that are lucky enough to survive attacks of innumerable enemies and other hazards settle down on a clean, smooth, hard rocky or shelly surface where they become permanently fixed by means of a byssus and never move again. Oyster breeding consists largely in providing suitable surfaces for the 'spat' to settle on. In England quantities of clean shell,

Fig. 27: Oysters

A. The Saddle Oyster: *Anomia epihippum* × 1 nat. size approx. B. The Common European or Native Oyster: *Ostrea edulis*, fixed to a rock × 1 nat. size. C. The Portuguese Oyster: *Crassostrea angulata* × ½ nat. size approx. D. The American or Blue Point Oyster: *Crassostrea virginica* × ½ nat. size approx.

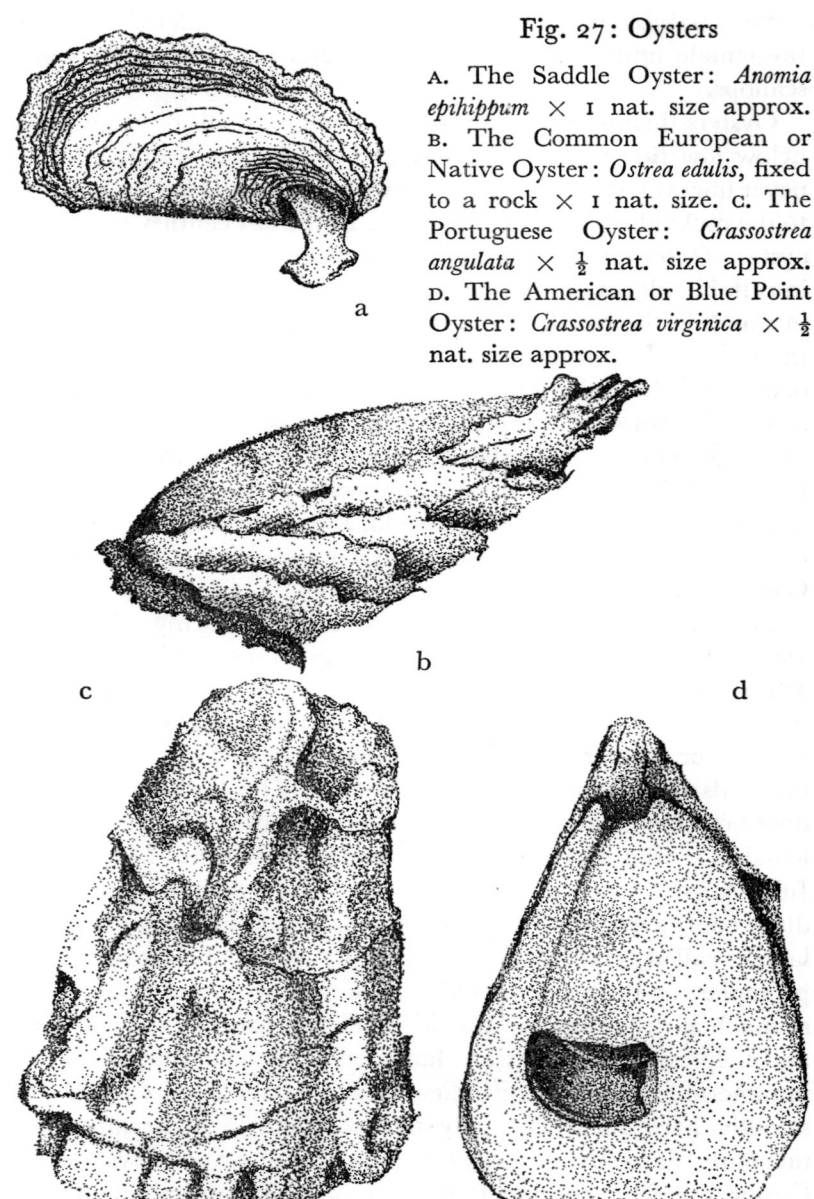

a

b

c

d

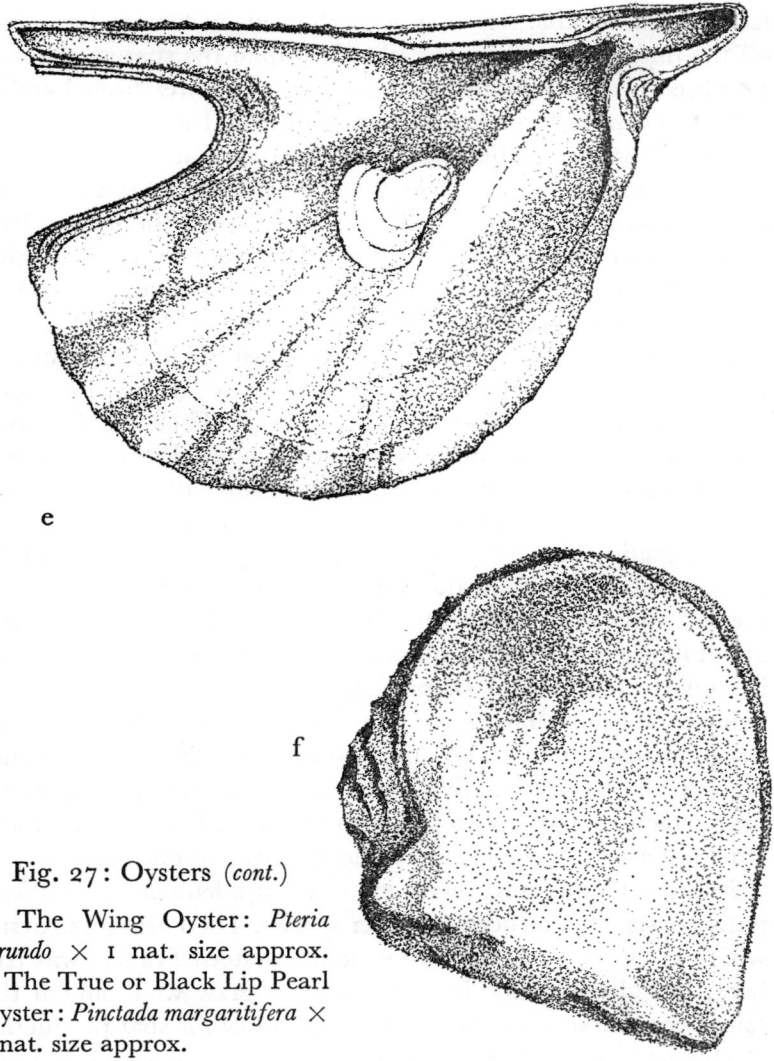

e

f

Fig. 27: Oysters (*cont.*)

E. The Wing Oyster: *Pteria hirundo* × 1 nat. size approx.
F. The True or Black Lip Pearl Oyster: *Pinctada margaritifera* × ½ nat. size approx.

called 'cultch', are scattered over the bottom of the beds. In France, where the breeding of oysters is done on a much bigger scale, the collectors are roofing tiles painted with a mixture of

7

lime and sand. When the young oysters have grown on the collectors to a suitable size they are removed, in France by flaking off the lime coating from the tiles. In Japan the spat are allowed to settle on empty oyster shells hanging by wires from bamboo rafts, or even on branches of bamboo planted in the sand. After removal from the collectors the oysters are fattened in special shallow ponds of sea water warmed by the sun so as to produce an abundance of plant life (diatoms) on which the oysters feed. At Arcachon this plant life is so rich and abundant that it gives the oysters a greenish tinge which is supposed to be specially delectable and, of course, adds to their price.

When the young oyster first settles down on its hard substratum, or on its collector, it searches about with its foot for a little while looking for a place to cement itself. Then the foot soon disappears and a cementing substance is poured from the byssus gland, fixing the oyster to the substratum with the left valve underneath and the right valve uppermost. The native oyster (*Ostrea edulis*—Fig. 27b) is very inequivalve with the lower left valve much larger than the upper right one and curved so that the flat right valve sits within it like a lid. The native oyster is about four to six inches in diameter (hinge to margin) and usually irregularly rounded in shape. The rounded shape of the lower valve is often misshapen and distorted so as to conform with the irregularities of the surface upon which it is lying. The brownish outer surface of the native oyster shell is marked by irregular lines which correspond to periods of growth. Only one adductor (the posterior) remains and it is mostly this that one eats.

Many attempts have been made to supplement our stocks of native oysters by introducing other species. The Portuguese oyster, which grows very successfully in south-western France, was tried here, but although the imported oysters grew well enough they found the temperature of our waters too low for spat production. Portuguese oysters are still imported and fattened here but cannot be bred. American blue point oysters were also tried but the same was found to be true, though their pests flourished.

The Portuguese oyster (*Crassostrea angulata*—Fig. 27c) is a much broader, deeper shell than the native oyster, more trough-shaped with a crenellated margin. It is often distorted and irregular in shape and may reach a width of seven inches from hinge to margin. It is dirty white, cream or light brown in colour with a brown periostracum. There are concentric ridges on the outside of the shell and a few prominent radiating ribs. The valves are inequivalve with the larger left cupped and the upper smaller right valve flat.

The American blue point oyster (*C. virginica*—Fig. 27d) is not really a member of our fauna but a native of the eastern coast of the United States. It is a large shell, up to seven inches across, oval in outline and pointed towards the apex so that the shell is shaped like a tear-drop. The valves, again, are very inequivalve.

Returning to our rock faces below low tide we shall find the large horse mussel (*Modiolus modiolus*—Fig. 17a), as mentioned in Chapter 3, clinging to rock faces when mature but sheltering among Laminaria and other holdfasts when young. Empty horse mussel shells are often found cast up on the beach after rough weather. It is commoner around our northern than our southern coasts and grows up to a length of about six inches. It grows in a great belt in the Irish Sea around the Isle of Man. It is a dark purplish shell with the beaks not quite at the anterior end and nearer to the centre of the shell than those of the common mussel so that the shell has a less pointed shape. The young shell is covered with a horny mat of fibres, often having a spiny appearance entangling small stones and grains of sand. This is formed by the periostracum and wears off as the shell gets older.

In holes in the submerged rocks and in crevices, in holdfasts of strap and other weeds and in holes bored in the rocks by other molluscs, we may find the little gaper (*Sphenia binghami*—Fig. 25d). This is a very truncated, pale green, brown or yellow shell about half an inch long and roughly rectangular in shape. The valves are inequivalve, the right one slightly larger and more convex than the left which has the spoon-shaped chondrophore characteristic of all gapers. It lives attached inside its crack or crevice by means of a byssus.

If we now leave the rocks and dive overboard from a boat, gazing down through our goggling mask at a bottom of clean or muddy sand, we get the curious feeling that we are in a balloon sailing smoothly over a vast, flat desert plain. Starfish and brittle stars are splayed out inertly beneath us, the latter maybe in tangled masses, while here and there a little cloud of sand arises, like a conflagration viewed from our balloon, as a flatfish flaps away as we glide above. But we may be lucky and behold a much greater conflagration suddenly arise when a scallop claps its shell and leaps away. The famous and beautiful scallop shell is extremely common all round our coasts on sandy bottoms offshore. We have about a dozen different species all of which begin life attached by means of a byssus to rock or stone or shell, but while still quite small they lose their attachment and become free-swimming.

The great scallop or clam (*Pecten maximus*—Pl. 13) of our shores, whose rayed shell with lateral wings, reddish brown or yellow and four to five inches in diameter, is familiar to everybody, lies on its side as does the oyster. The valves are inequivalve but, unlike the oyster, the right valve is convex and lies underneath while the left valve is flat and lies on top. The anterior adductor muscle has quite disappeared but the posterior one is very much enlarged as in the oyster, and occupies a central position. Again, it is mainly this great adductor that is the edible portion of the shellfish. By the sudden contraction of this powerful muscle the scallop is able to shut its valves abruptly. When the muscle is relaxed the powerful ligament between the hinge wings of the shell causes the valves to fly open again. The scallop does not move about much but prefers to lie in a shallow bed in the sand which it makes for itself by repeatedly flapping its valves until the flat upper left valve is just level with the surface of the sand. When disturbed it can shoot off in any direction it likes by clapping its valves together. The edges of the mantle are reinforced by muscular curtains just inside the valve margins, and they are apposed to one another, but by leaving a gap between them in any position and clapping its valves together smartly the scallop can expel a jet of water through the gap and move off by jet propulsion in the direction opposite to the gap. The upper marginal curtains overlap the lower ones so that the jet of water is directed

downwards when the scallop claps its valves with the result that
the shell tends to jump upwards and moves in a series of arcs.
Normally, when the scallop claps its valves together, the direction
of motion is, somewhat unexpectedly, such that the free valve
margins are forward. This is because in normal progression it
expels water through gaps in the mantle margin immediately
in front of and behind the hinge line, that is, on either side of
the hinge line and wings when the shell is looked at full on. But
in an emergency the scallop can move in any other direction or
with the hinge line forward by adjusting the positions of the gaps
between the mantle margins through which it expels the jet.

Most bivalves, owing to their sedentary habits, have lost all
external sense organs, but the scallop, by reason of having secondarily developed a mobile habit, has also secondarily acquired
sense organs. The edges of the mantle are armed with a fringe of
sensory tentacles and between the tentacles are eyes. Each of
these eyes, though not really comparable with those of vertebrates,
nevertheless has a retina and a well formed lens and each is
supplied by a nerve, all quite independently developed. Probably
these organs do not do much more than perceive differences of
light and shadow, but since there is a lens it is possible that they
may be able to distinguish shapes.

The great scallop is common on sandy bottoms offshore all
round the coasts of the British Isles and there are commercial
fisheries for it off the east and south-east coasts since, after the
oyster, it is the aristocrat of shellfish. It is taken in light trawls
because, being so mobile and active, it can easily hop out of the
way of a dredge. The shells of all our species of scallop are cast
up on the beach from time to time and at the very lowest spring
tides the living animal itself may sometimes be exposed.

The small many-ribbed tiger scallop (*Chlamys tigerina*—Fig.
28a), not more than one and a quarter inches in diameter, has
wings of different sizes, the anterior ones being three times larger
than the posterior. The shells may be of many colours from purple
to yellow with blotches, streaks and zig-zag markings. It is common
from very low down between the tide marks out to fifty fathoms,
under stones and in crevices.

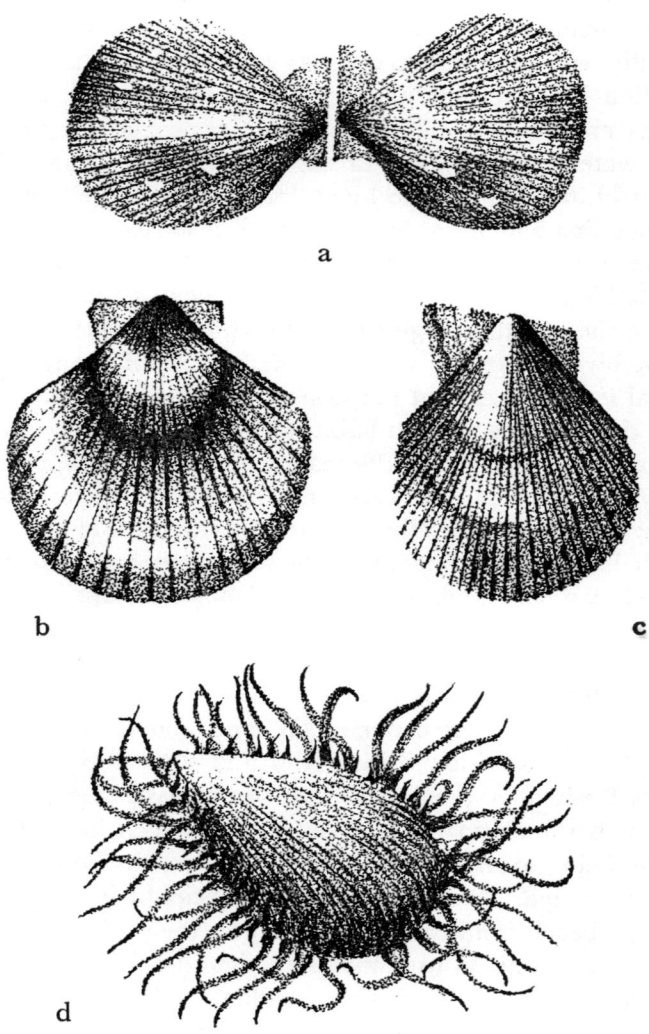

Fig. 28: Scallops

A. The Tiger Scallop: *Chlamys tigerina* × 1 nat. size approx. B. The Queen Scallop: *Chlamys opercularis* × 1 nat. size approx. C. The Variegated Scallop: *Chlamys varia* × ¾ nat. size approx. D. The Gaping File Shell: *Lima hians* × 1 nat. size

The hunchback scallop (*C. distorta*) has a similar distribution but it is not free living. After attaching itself by a byssus it becomes cemented to a rock or stone, right valve downwards. When young the shell is round but after becoming cemented it grows lop-sided and becomes inequivalve with the lower right valve more convex than the left upper one.

The queen scallop (*C. opercularis*—Fig. 28b) is the most beautiful of all the scallops and may be rose pink, purple, orange, or yellow, or any of those tints all together in irregular patterns. It is about half the size of the great scallop and inequivalve, with the left, upper valve becoming progressively more convex as the shell grows older. It is attached by a byssus when young and then becomes free-living. Queen scallops are very active and move about over the bottom in shoals, often in great numbers. They used to be very common in the Firth of Forth where they lived in some kind of association with the horse mussel which probably provided them with a firm attachment for their byssus threads. Unfortunately these scallop beds are nowadays greatly diminished.

The variegated scallop (*C. varia*—Fig. 28c) is oval in shape with very asymmetrical wings and its ribs are covered with blunt-ended processes. It lives either free or attached by a byssus from very low down on the shore out to about forty-five fathoms.

In the tropics, especially in the Pacific, among coral reefs there lives a large and variegated family of bivalves, the thorny oysters (Spondylidae), related to our scallops but with the shells bearing very many long spines and processes. The shells often grow very big, up to ten inches across. They live permanently fixed by a byssus among the coral growths and their numerous spines and projections become so encrusted with other accretions that they are often very difficult to see. When the encrusting growths are removed and the shells carefully cleaned they are seen to have brilliant colours, often rose pink or purple.

The gaping file shell (*Lima hians*—Fig. 28d) of our offshore waters belongs to another family (Limidae) closely related to the scallops. It lives from extreme low water to about fifty-five fathoms usually on stony, gravelly bottoms. It makes a nest for itself among the stones or in holdfasts by binding together stones, bits of weed and other rubbish by means of its byssus threads. The nest may be occupied by one shell or by an adult and several young ones and has separate holes for the entrance and exit of sea water. It is probable that the nests have a protective function since the file shell would be extremely vulnerable and helpless outside the nest. The edges of its mantle are produced into two fringes of long orange or red sensory tentacles which cannot be withdrawn into the valves but perpetually wave and explore around their edges. The valves gape perpetually (hence the name) with these tentacles extremely conspicuous so that the file shell is a sitting target for any enemy, especially fish. It can, however, move about and does so in a series of languid hops, like the scallop but less vigorously. The valves are held vertically during flight through the water whereas the scallop holds the valves horizontally. At each leap the file shell's tentacles wave in the water like crimson tresses. The delicate valves are pure white, rhombohedral in shape with rounded angles. With its crimson or orange tentacles protruding between the white valves the file shell is a very lovely object.

The scallop shell has been loved and venerated by western civilization since ancient times, largely on account of its exquisite and classic shape which has been adopted as an important feature in architecture and design for many centuries. For the ancient Greeks the scallop shell was the symbol of the sea. Aphrodite (Venus to the Romans), the goddess of love and beauty, arose from the sea fully formed out of a scallop shell and it is on a scallop shell that she is depicted being wafted towards the shore in Botticelli's wonderful picture 'The Birth of Venus'. Titian painted Venus Anadyomene arising from the waves with a scallop shell in the background. The earliest example of a scallop shell used in design is on a Greek vase found on the shores of the Black Sea dating from 400 B.C. Since then scallop shells have proliferated in architecture, design and painting right up to the eighteenth century. The scallop depicted in Greek and Roman painting and design was the Mediterranean scallop (*Pecton jacobaeus*) which is seen on early Phoenician coins. Pliny observed it and recorded its movements, and its remains have been unearthed in a collection of shells at Pompeii. Later, still in its role as a symbol of the sea, the scallop shell became the symbol of St James the Apostle who was a fisherman. To this day he is the patron saint of Spain, for legend has it that after the Ascension he went to Spain and evangelized that country and was buried, after many adventures, in the city of Santiago de Compostela in north-western Spain. How the scallop shell became attached to his name is not known but one legend relates how he saved a horseman from drowning at Padron, the seaport of Santiago. When the horseman was brought ashore he and his horse were covered with scallop shells which are abundant in the sea off Padron. Whatever the origin of the symbol may be, the scallop shell became the badge of pilgrims to the shrine of St James at Compostela and was worn as a sign that they had made the pilgrimage, the third most important in Christendom. At one time the sale of scallop shells anywhere except at Compostela was forbidden under pain of excommunication. The scallop shell is a device which appears on the coats of arms of many old English families and sometimes, though not always, signifies a pilgrimage to the shrine of St James.

In the middle of the nineteenth century shell boxes and shell ornaments, often using the scallop shell as a centre piece, became fashionable in England. Shells were worn as jewellery. The brothers Marcus and Samuel Samuel started a business importing shells for this purpose from all over the world. When paraffin lamps came in they started a sideline importing kerosene, and this became considerably more than a sideline when the internal combustion engine came on the scene so that the import of shells rather faded out. The brothers took to dealing in oil but kept a shell as their symbol. First of all they used the rayed tellin (*Tellina donacina*) and then, at the beginning of this century, adopted the St James's scallop. This is now a familiar sign on all our roads and on the funnels of oil tankers on all the oceans of the world as the trade mark of the great international oil combine which developed from the import of ornamental shells not much more than a hundred years ago.

The scallop's Latin scientific name, *Pecten*—a comb—refers to its resemblance to the comb which Spanish ladies wear in their hair. Alternatively it may be that the comb which Spanish women wear is, in fact, the scallop shell, the symbol of their country's patron saint.

There are innumerable other bivalves on sandy and muddy bottoms below low tide and they are mostly immobile but can be brought up with a dredge. It is impossible to deal with them all within the compass of a small book so that I shall only mention the more important and striking among them.

There are several large venus shells such as the warty venus (*Venus verrucosa*), a very solid shell with concentric ridges bearing tubercles. The blunt tellin (*Tellina crassa*), yellowish with pink rays, and the large sunset shell (*Gari depressa*), also yellowish with fainter pink rays, both burrow in sand offshore.

The most famous and abundant of the trough shells occurs below low tide out to fairly deep water. This is the cut trough shell (*Spisula subtruncata*) which lives in incredible abundance on the Dogger Bank in the North Sea and there forms the principal food of the plaice and other flatfishes which migrate to the bank in great numbers in order to feed on it. It is smaller than the thick trough (*S. solida*—Fig. 21c) found on the sandy shore along the low tide mark and has the shape of a more elongated triangle with rounded angles.

The rayed trough shell (*Mactra corallina*) is common on bottoms of clean sand and has a smooth solid shell, up to two inches long, with brown rays from umbo to margin on a white creamy ground.

The prickly cockle (*Acanthocardia echinata*) inhabits fine sand, gravel or mud from about two fathoms out to deep water. It has about twenty radiating ribs with broad spines on them connected by raised crests. The shell is about three inches long. There are also several other rarer cockles on offshore bottoms.

The family of the astarte shells, of which the best known is *Astarte triangularis* (Fig. 29a), all live offshore, usually in sand or gravel but also sometimes in mud. They are solid shells, not much more than an inch long, with concentric ridges. *A. triangularis*, as its name implies, is triangular in outline while the other members of the family are rounded or oval.

The family of the nut shells, too, (Nuculidae) is very abundant on sandy bottoms offshore. Nut shells are mostly olive brown or yellowish in colour, irregularly oval in outline and seldom more than three-quarters of an inch in length. There are about six species not easy to distinguish from one another. They often cover the bottom in great numbers and are remarkable in that they collect their food by means of the flaps (labial palps) on either side of the mouth.

On offshore bottoms of true mud there are several remarkable shells whose empty valves may sometimes be found cast up on the beach, Firstly, there are the wing oysters and fan mussels. The wing oysters are very closely related to the pearl oyster which is more closely related to the mussel than to the native oyster itself. Pearl oysters live mainly in the Persian Gulf and Red Sea (see p. 137) and our representative of the family is the much humbler but nonetheless beautiful wing oyster (*Pteria hirundo*— Fig. 27e). It is so called because the valves are produced fore and aft into two ears or wings. The shell is very inequilateral and the umbo is far forward. In front of the umbo a rounded triangular process or ear projects forward with a byssal notch below it. Behind the umbo the margins of the valves are produced backwards horizontally to form a long, narrow, pointed posterior ear. Underneath the straight horizontal line of this wing the shell rather resembles an oyster in shape and appearance, rounded and pearly inside and about three inches across. The outside of the shell is brown and roughened with tiny warts. Wing oysters live in sandy mud attached by a byssus which protrudes through a considerable gape under the anterior ear.

The fan mussel (*Pinna fragilis*—Fig. 17b) is not really related to the true edible mussel but is more closely related to the wing oyster and so to the mussel at one remove. It is an exceedingly inequilateral shell with the umbo and articulation far forward. In front of the umbo the forward margin of the valve forms a narrow point. Backwards the two valves widen out to the fan-shaped posterior end of the shell so that the general shape is that of an isosceles triangle with rounded corners. The base of the triangle, which is the posterior margin of the shell, is curved slightly and so is the dorsal margin of the shell. The shell is brown

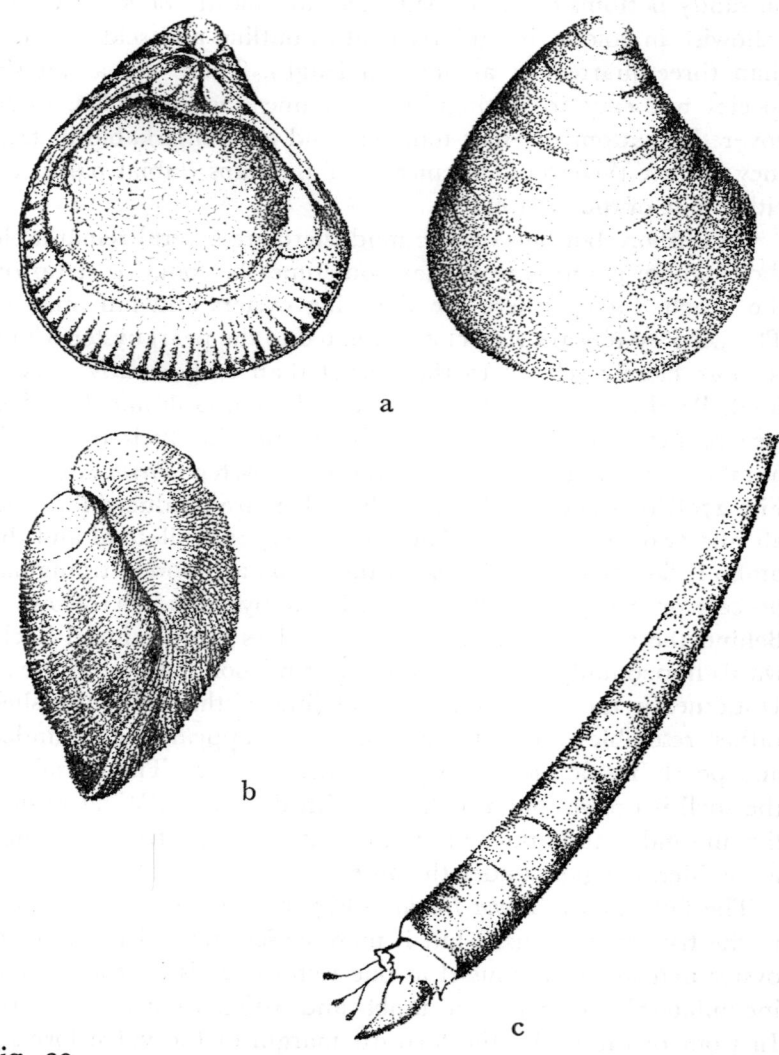

Fig. 29

A. *Astarte triangularis* × 15 nat. size approx. Actual length, ant. to post. margin, rarely more than $\frac{1}{8}$th inch. B. The Basket shell: *Corbula gibba* × 2 nat. size approx. C. The Elephant's Tusk shell: *Dentalium entalis* × $2\frac{1}{2}$ nat. size approx.

in colour and curiously fragile, as its name implies, so that one can easily break bits off the posterior margin with the fingers. Like the wing oyster the fan mussel lies buried in mud, attached to stones by a byssus which passes out under the pointed anterior end. The sharp curved posterior edges of the valves just project above the surface of the mud as the mussel sits, pointed end downward, with the valves apart. The fan mussel is the largest of the British bivalves and may reach a length of a foot from the anterior point to the posterior margin; in tropical waters fan mussels may reach twice that length. They are a practical argument, if one were needed, for always wearing shoes when hunting on the beach. For though they often live at considerable depths, they do not always do so and large beds of them are found on mud flats within paddling range in shallow water, though they are never uncovered. With their razor-sharp curved edges just above the mud they are a real menace, resembling the Indian fakir's bed of knives.

Secondly, in addition to these, there is the basket shell, (*Corbula gibba*—Fig. 29b), one of the commonest shells offshore usually in muddy sand. In some areas it occurs in great numbers. It is a solid, rounded, white shell about half an inch in diameter with very unequal valves. The right valve is very much larger and more convex than the left which fits firmly and snugly into it. The outer margin of the smaller left valve is fringed by a soft, grey, uncalcified, horny curtain of periostracum rather like a draught excluder. This makes a snug union between the margin of the small left valve and that of the overlapping right. The left valve has about half a dozen radiating ribs which are absent from the right one. Both valves have many concentric ridges.

Most shells which are markedly inequivalve, as we saw in the oyster and the scallop, lie on their sides with one valve or other underneath. The basket shell, however, burrows vertically into the sand with its anterior end downwards, as in fact most burrowing bivalves do. The burrowing is done by means of the very long foot which is tubular and worms its way down into the sand until the shell is buried vertically with only its short siphons flush with the surface. The foot has a fine groove underneath it running to the tip. Down this the byssal secretion travels and anchors the shell to a stone by means of a fine thread, after which the basket shell does not move again.

Only two mud-burrowing snails live offshore. They are found to considerable depths but seldom between the tide marks although their cast-up empty shells are very common on beaches of muddy

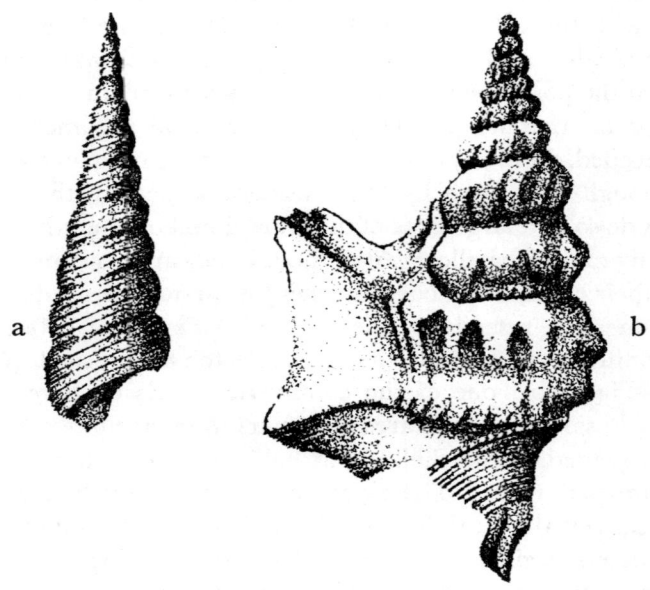

Fig. 30

A. The Common Tower shell: *Turritella communis* × 2 nat. size approx.
B. The Pelican's Foot snail: *Aporrhais pes-pelecani* × 1½ nat. size approx.

sand and are therefore quite familiar objects to wanderers on the shore. They are both remarkable among gastropods for being suspension or deposit feeders.

One is the common tower shell (*Turritella communis*—Fig. 30a) which lives offshore burrowing into thick, compact, muddy gravel by means of its foot. It lies motionless all its life unless disturbed, drawing water down to itself through an inhalent shaft which it excavates in the mud, and out again by a separate exhalent shaft. The two shafts are lined by mucus which the animal secretes as does the land snail and the current is caused by cilia which line the gills. The animal relies for its food on the fine particles suspended in the inhalent stream.

The other mud-burrowing snail is the pelican's foot snail (*Aporrhais pes-pelecani*—Fig. 30b), which is also a tower-shaped shell with about ten ornamented and sculptured whorls. The outer margin or lip of the aperture is produced outwards in older shells to form a wing with several processes or digitations supposedly resembling a pelican's foot. This snail also lies buried just below the surface in sandy mud offshore with an inhalent and exhalent shaft lined by mucus and made by the siphons. It differs from the tower shell in having no cilia on the gills but the current is drawn into the mantle cavity, as in any other marine coiled snail, by rhythmical contractions of the muscles which line the walls of the mantle cavity, and is therefore purely respiratory. The siphon tube extends up the inhalent burrow and searches the surface of the mud, drawing down in the respiratory current the fine deposit to the snail below. The pelican's foot snail is thus a true deposit feeder while the common tower shell is a ciliary suspension feeder. It is a lonely British representative of a large and illustrious tropical family, the large and beautiful conch shells (Strombidae). Many of the big tropical shells belonging to this family move about by lifting up their shells and then falling forward so as to progress by means of a series of jerks, and it may be from this that our small and humble pelican's foot snail evolved its burrowing habit.

Finally we come to the tusk shells which belong to a different class of molluscs altogether, the Scaphopoda, in many ways intermediate between gastropods and bivalves. As explained in chapter one the shell and mantle have become a tube by the fusion of the two halves which are separate in youth. The tube is wider at one end than at the other, and, from the wide end, a trilobed foot projects with which the animal burrows into the sand. The mouth is also at the wider end and is surrounded by a fringe of fine filaments which are used for feeding. The narrow end of the tube projects above the surface of the sand and an inhalent current is drawn in through its opening and out again at the wider lower opening. The mantle is ciliated and functions instead of a gill. Tusk shells are commoner off our northern than our southern shores and are never found between the tide marks. There is only one common species, the elephant tusk shell (*Dentalium entalis*—Fig. 29c), which has a slightly curved, white tubular shell like an elephant's tusk on a minute scale. It is about an inch long and quite solidly built. Another rarer species (*D. tarentinum*) has longitudinal grooving on the shell.

Plate 9. Mussels (*Mytilus galloprovincialis*) with limpets and barnacles. *Photo: Douglas P. Wilson, FRPS.*

Plate 10. Soft bubble shells (*Akera bullata*) swimming. Note the apical filament of the specimen on the right. *Photo: Douglas P. Wilson, FRPS.*

7

BORERS IN ROCK AND WOOD

SOME bivalves have taken to boring into rock or into wood. In order to collect these we shall probably have to use the crude method of the hammer and chisel, but we must go about it very carefully because the shells of these tunnelling bivalves are extremely delicate, and in most cases the burrow, and the animal inside it, are deceptively larger than the opening of the burrow indicates. Besides these bivalve molluscs there are many other marine animals which tunnel into rock, and some which tunnel into wood. A sea urchin makes shallow round cavities in rocks and there are small worms which make U-shaped burrows from which little tubes of mud project. But the carefully and accurately excavated, rounded tunnels drilled by bivalves are unmistakable and are found mainly along the low tide mark.

In all our British rock-boring bivalves it is the shell itself which is used as a tunnelling tool. It tunnels so efficiently that many observers have expressed the opinion that there must be some chemical action at work. However, this is not so. The only bivalve which uses a chemical is the date mussel (*Lithophagus lithophagus*), which lives in the Mediterranean and in the tropics. It uses an acid secreted by a special gland and this eats away the limestone into which the bivalve tunnels. The date mussel, so called because it is about the size of a date and looks rather like one, protects itself from the action of its own acid by developing a very thick tough outer layer of periostracum while the shelly layer itself is very thin. All the rock borers of our coasts, using the shell only, tunnel into soft rocks—sandstone, chalk, sometimes limestone. They also tunnel into stiff clay and peat and occasionally into wood. The Devon and Dorset coasts, but not the coast of Cornwall which is made of granite, are therefore the best areas in which to look for borers.

From a study of the 'rednose' (*Hiatella striata*—Fig. 31a) it is possible to understand how the tunnelling habit might perhaps have arisen among bivalves, for it tunnels only into the very softest rock and often, indeed, does not tunnel at all but merely nestles in a hole or crevice, among mussels or among weed holdfasts. In all such places it holds on by means of a byssus, but it is not quite certain how the rednose in fact does its tunnelling for it does not seem to use either the foot, which is very small, or the byssus while doing so, nor is there any chemical action involved. It is believed that the animal takes in water through the inhalent siphon, closes the openings of the siphons and then contracts the walls of the siphon tubes, which are very muscular. Thus it inflates the gill cavity with water like a bladder, forcing the valves of the shell apart against the rock. The exhalent opening then relaxes, letting the water out, deflating the bladder of the gill cavity and allowing the valves to return to their former position. The animal does not actually start tunnelling unless it is already lodged in a convenient hole or crevice. This sounds a most laborious method of working but nevertheless the rednose is able to bore deep and well cut burrows. It gets its name from the fact that the strong muscular siphons, which are separated only at the tip and which project a little way from the entrance to the burrow, are pink in colour. The shell is white, irregular in shape though as a rule roughly rectangular, and about one and a half inches long. The valves gape posteriorly to accommodate the siphons.

On our south and south-west coasts the commonest rock borer is the piddock (*Pholas dactylus*—Fig. 31b), which always lives in a tunnel and bores into everything except the hardest rocks. It will bore into any sedimentary rock and into schists, and also into submerged wood, clay or peat. The shell, which reaches a length of about three inches in large specimens, is elongated, white and rather delicate but extremely hard. At the anterior end it bears fifty longitudinal rows of spines, each spine situated at the intersection of one of the concentric ridges with one of the radial ribs. The valves gape apart widely at both ends. At the posterior end they accommodate the immense siphon which may be three times the length of the shell itself and bifurcates into inhalent and exhalent portions where it projects from the burrow. The burrow itself may be as much as a foot deep. At the front end of the shell the valves gape to allow for the very powerful foot which is reinforced with special muscles attached to additional plates on the upper margin of the shell between the valves. The valves of the piddock are specially modified in connection with their function as a tunnelling tool. There is no ligament between them and the articulating teeth common to most bivalves are replaced by a rounded ball on each valve so that a ball joint is formed on which the valves can rock.

The piddock burrows by grinding away the rock with the toothed front end of its shell. It takes a firm grip with its foot which can adhere to the rock like a sucker by the contraction of its powerful muscles. At first the foot adheres to the rock surface and then, later, to the inside of the tunnel. The rock is ground away by the oscillation of the valves on their ball joint and this movement is imparted to them by anterior and posterior adductor muscles which contract alternately. As the animal bores down into the rock it changes the position of its foot so as to allow its shell drill to play from many different angles. In this way accurate, straight holes with a smooth rounded bore are tunnelled into the rock. They are usually wider at the inner end than at the outer because the animal grows in size as it ceaselessly and tirelessly grinds away throughout its life. Thus the aperture from which the siphons project is of much narrower bore than the part occupied by the shell. In rocks crowded with piddocks the tunnels often intersect because each animal bores relentlessly straight on in the direction it has chosen and burrows of neighbours often join and cross. Indeed it has been recorded that a piddock bored unnoting through the body of another that was in its way. The animal is not attached inside its burrow so that if a piddock is removed from its tunnel and placed on a suitable rock surface it can start boring all over again.

Like all borers the piddock is a suspension feeder but rejects the spoilage from its own tunnel, casting it out through the exhalent siphon. A strange feature of this animal, which spends all

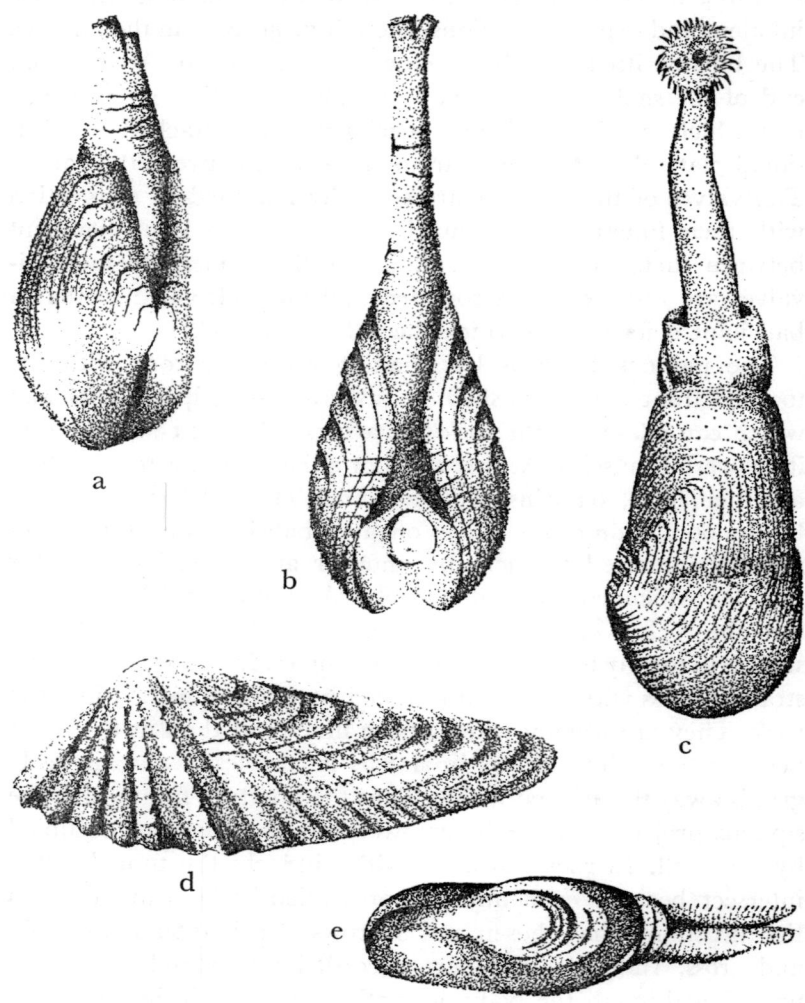

Fig. 31 : Rock borers

A. The Red Nose: *Hiatella striata* × 1 nat. size. B. The Common Piddock: *Pholas dactylus* × 1 nat. size. C. The Paper Piddock: *Pholadidea loscombiana* × 1 nat. size. D. The American Piddock: *Petricola pholadiformis* × 2 nat. size. E. The Flask shell: *Gastrochaena dubia* × 2 nat. size its life laboriously grinding away in its tunnel, is that it is one of the most brilliantly phosphorescent of marine animals. On extraction from its burrow the whole surface of the body glows with a bright greenish blue light.

There are several other piddocks around our coasts besides the common one. The oval piddock (*Zirphaea crispata*) is slightly larger, about three and a half inches long. The shell is coarse and heavy-looking and the front end, carrying about twenty rows of teeth is triangular in outline. The valves are white but covered with a brown periostracum and the joined siphon tubes are very large. It usually burrows into clay, peat, shale or soft rock.

The white piddock (*Barnea candida*—Pl. 14) is smaller than the common piddock (about two and a half inches long) and bores into similar materials. It has only a single extra plate on the upper part of the shell between the valves instead of the four which the common piddock possesses.

The little piddock (*B. parva*) is smaller still, about one and a half inches long. The solidly built shell is much cut away in front and the abrasive surface is provided by prominent scale-like radiating ridges.

While the two larger piddocks occur from extreme low tide out to three or four fathoms, the white and little piddocks are found from mid-shore downwards to a few fathoms out to sea. They are versatile borers, tunnelling into everything except crystalline rock, even into cement.

The paper piddock (*Pholadidea loscombiana*—Fig. 31c) is found only on our south-western coasts and differs considerably from the others. It is immediately recognizable by the membranous cup at the base of the siphon tube from which it gets its name and into which siphons can be withdrawn. In young animals the white valves, covered with a yellowish periostracum, gape to accommodate the foot. When the animal is full grown it stops burrowing and spends the rest of its life sitting placidly in its burrow, suspension feeding. The foot then atrophies and disappears and the gape between the valves which accommodated it closes by the ingrowth of the tissues around it. The scar where the gape was becomes covered by an external horny layer. As a rule the paper piddock bores only into the softest materials.

The American piddock (*Petricola pholadiformis*—Fig. 31d) is not really related to the piddocks at all but has similar habits. It is, in fact more closely related to the venus shells. The shell, about two inches long, resembles that of a piddock with ridges and spines, but there are no extra plates dorsally between the valves, and the siphons are separate. The off-white coloured valves are very inequilateral with the umbo pronounced, very turned down and placed well forward. There are about forty radiating ribs, those on the front part of the shell being the most pronounced.

The American piddock bores into clay, chalk, mud or limestone and is found between the tidemarks mostly on our east coasts, especially the coast of Essex and in the Thames estuary. This, again, is another of the additions to our fauna brought over from America, presumably during the eighties of the last century as a consequence of attempts to introduce the Blue Point Oyster to our shores. The American piddock was first reported in the River Crouch in July 1890 and now has a distribution from the coast of Lincolnshire to that of Dorset and has been reported in the River Fal in Cornwall.

The flask shell (*Gastrochaena dubia*—Fig. 31e) gets its name from the shape of the excavation it makes. The shell is smooth and there are no additional plates between the upper margins of the valves. The siphons are joined together yet distinct, that is to say they are not united by a horny sheath, but the animal secretes limy tubes around them inside the burrow. The flask shell tunnels into all but the very hardest rocks and sometimes into the shells of other molluscs.

The rock-boring bivalves only occasionally tunnel into wood and then usually only if it is soft and water-logged. There are, however, one or two notorious bivalves which regularly bore into wood and not into rock and have on this account been a great problem and nuisance to mankind for centuries.

The most famous, or perhaps notorious, of the wood-boring bivalves is the shipworm (*Nototeredo norvagicus*—Fig. 32a—and

Teredo navalis), two common species in our waters which regularly attack the submerged timbers of ships, boats and wooden piles if they are not protected in some way. Unlike the rock borers, the shipworm actually devours and ingests the wood which it gnaws out to form its burrow, using it as food and excreting the digested material into the exhalent current. Looking at boat timbers or jetty piles infected with shipworm it is often impossible to see more from the outside than a peppering of small rounded shot-holes not much larger than those made by the common furniture beetle. In many cases, however, little is left but the shell of the timber which is honeycombed inside with channels running along the grain, having the diameter of a man's finger and lined with shelly material laid down by the worms themselves. In many cases the wood is so fragile that it breaks easily away leaving these shelly linings standing up by themselves. Some of the burrows may be as much as a foot long and they never intersect or run into one another. Unlike the piddock the shipworm, by some unknown means, carefully avoids interfering with its neighbours. If, during the course of its excavations, a shipworm encounters another burrow it stops short, seals its burrow with a shelly lining and starts off again in another direction.

The shipworm sheds its eggs and sperm into the sea through its exhalent siphon. Like the oyster and the slipper limpet it undergoes a sex change as it grows older, but, unlike them, it is first male and then female. The eggs are fertilized in the water outside the burrow and the burrows are so crowded together in an infected piece of wood that this is easily enough achieved. Clouds of tiny bivalve larvae result which drift about with the tides and currents for months. Those lucky enough to settle at last on a piece of wood cling on temporarily by means of a single byssus thread but soon start to tunnel actively into the wood itself. The place of settling does not seem to be entirely a matter of luck for there seems to be some sort of chemical attraction towards wood. A solution of wood in alcohol is found to have a similar attractive power. During the several months of their larval life young shipworms may be carried far out to sea so that there is always a very good chance of any unprotected piece of timber or floating driftwood becoming infected, no matter how far out it may be.

Once the little larva is inside its pinhole burrow great changes set in and growth takes place very rapidly. The valves lose their purely protective role and become thickened and hard so as to form a highly efficient boring instrument, but they remain very small in comparison with the rest of the body of the animal. The shell develops five separate parts, the two anterior and largest plates having about a hundred serrated ridges which form the abrasive surface and do the actual boring. They do it by rocking backward and forwards on a ball articulation as do the valves of piddock. The shell is white or light brown with a brown periostracum but does not nearly contain the body of the animal. In our largest shipworm, *Nototeredo norvagicus*, the shell is about a quarter of an inch in diameter and as it bores down into the wood the long, soft body elongates behind it, filling the burrow. This worm-like body contains all the organs of the mollusc and lines the burrow as it grows with a shelly wall of its own secretion. The animal works by attaching its foot by suction to the head of the burrow, as the piddock does, and rocking the serrated plates of its shell backwards and forwards through the contraction of the posterior adductor, forcing the anterior lobes of the shell apart, alternating with the contraction of the much smaller anterior adductor which draws them together again. Thus the serrated anterior plates of the shell are continually grinding at the wood inside the burrow while the foot keeps shifting its position so that the shell moves slowly through 180° while tunnelling, producing a smooth round tunnel considerably wider in diameter than the shell itself. It was from a study of the methods of the shipworm that Sir Marc Isambard Brunel, father of Isambard Kingdom Brunel, designed the rotary shield with which tunnels are bored to this day.

As the shipworm grows with its burrow the siphons remain attached to the relatively minute entrance. As the body grows in length it also at the same time grows in diameter so that the burrow from its small entrance enlarges downwards. Two small limy plates on either side of the siphons, actuated by special muscles, close the entrance like a pair of trap doors when the siphons are withdrawn. They are called the 'pallets' and ensure that when the entrance to the burrow is exposed to the air and the timbers left high and dry by the tide enough water is entrapped in the burrow for the worms to continue breathing. Shipworms in timbers of ships and boats can thus stay active for weeks when the vessel is in dry dock or hauled up on a slipway. When the burrow is submerged the trap doors open against the wall of the entrance and the two narrow siphons project outside. The exhalent siphon pours out a continuous stream of wood remains which have been digested in the alimentary canal. Since the shipworm is firmly attached at the entrance to its burrow it cannot be removed without damage and cannot make another burrow. It grows extremely rapidly but is quite short-lived, making a burrow about a foot long during a life of about eight months.

The shipworm was known to the Ancients, of course, and the Athenians coated their 'wooden walls' with plates of lead. In the middle ages and until the eighteenth century iron and copper were used to sheath the timbers of ships. In spite of this the damage done by the shipworm must have been enormous and Drake's *Golden Hind* foundered at her final anchorage in the Thames as a result of infestation with shipworm. Metal sheaths have never been very successful as an antidote because the slightest damage to the sheath, the corner of a plate turned up or a seam opened for a short distance, is enough to give the tiny larvae access to the wood beneath. Sheathing in concrete was adopted and usually used for underwater piles. It would hardly be suitable for ships or boats. Another method was 'scupper nailing'. A large number of broad headed nails were driven into the surface of the wood over the whole of the exposed area. The film of rust which spreads from the nail heads is inimical to the shipworm, but the method is not very effective and very laborious.

The shipworm is extremely sensitive to low salinities and is inhibited if the salinity of the water falls below ten parts per thousand and killed altogether if it falls below five parts per thousand. In Holland the timbers and sluices of dykes are usually immune from attack by shipworm except after periods of low rainfall when the salinity of the water increases above ten parts per thousand. Outbreaks of shipworm occur at these times which do great damage. It was as a result of a particularly serious one in 1730 that the Dutch government appointed the zoologist G. Snellius to investigate the shipworm and it is to him that we owe most of our knowledge about its methods and habits.

We have three different species of shipworm in our waters. The commonest and largest is *Nototeredo norvagicus* (Fig. 32a) which makes burrows up to a foot in length. The trapdoors or 'pallets' which guard the entrance to the burrow are shaped like tennis rackets. A second shipworm, *Teredo navalis*, is about half the size of *N. norvagicus* and has pallets shaped like tennis rackets notched at the tip. A third species, *Psiloteredo megotara*, is known as the drifting shipworm because it is usually found only on drift wood cast up on the shore. The pallets are shaped like tennis rackets with truncated ends. In tropical waters enormous shipworms occur which make burrows several yards long having the diameter of a man's arm.

Since the shipworm relies on wood for its food it is never found boring into any other material but there is another wood borer, the wood piddock (*Xylophaga dorsalis*—Fig. 32b) which, in spite of its name—meaning 'wood eater', does not eat the wood as it bores but, like the common piddock, merely tunnels into it for protection. Like the piddock too it is not attached to the entrance of its burrow and has no trap door 'pallets'. The shell is very much like that of a shipworm except that it encloses the whole body and only the siphons project behind. The wood piddock makes shallow rounded borings just under the surface of the wood with the bifurcate siphon tubes projecting from the entrance. The inhalent and exhalent siphons are joined except at their extremities. It attacks floating water-logged timber but has been known to bore into the insulation of submarine cables. Like the shipworm it undergoes sex change during its life, being first male and then becoming female, but it differs from the shipworm in that the sperm are retained within the mantle cavity and fertilize the eggs when the animal turns female, so that each animal is really self-fertilizing.

There are other wood-boring marine animals besides bivalve molluscs, and perhaps the most important and pestilential is the gribble, *Limnoria lignorum*. This is a crustacean and belongs to the great class of crustacea, the Isopoda, which includes the wood louse. It chews away, but does not digest, wood surfaces under water by means of the strong cutting blades (mandibles)

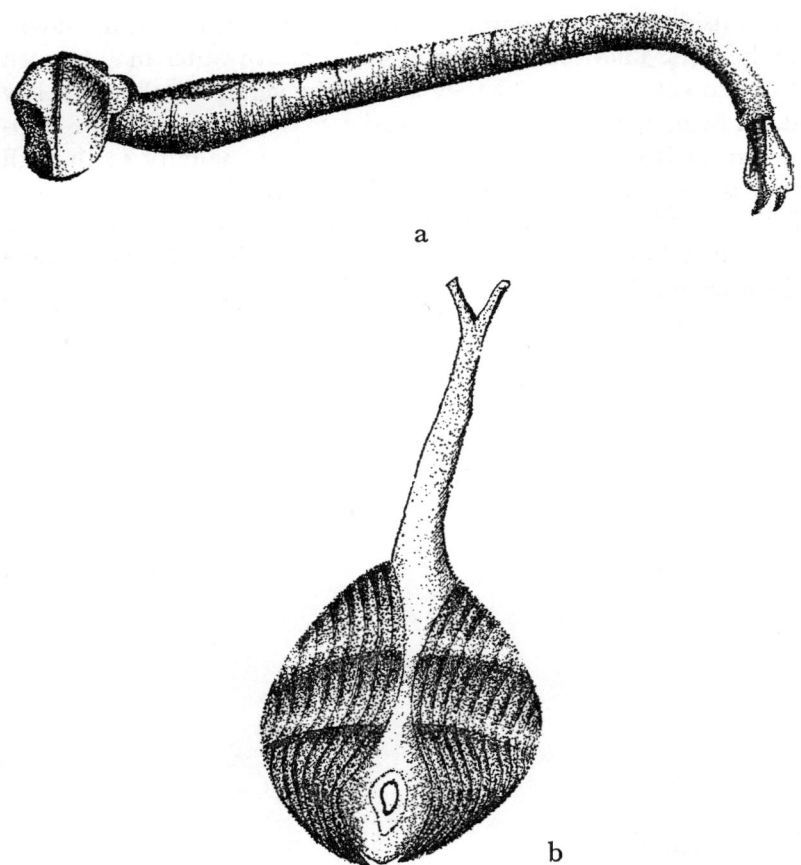

a

b

Fig. 32 : Wood borers

A. The Ship Worm: *Nototeredo norvagicus* × 1 nat. size. B. Wood Piddock: *Xylophaga dorsalis* × 2 nat. size approx.

on either side of its mouth. It makes shallow burrows under the surface of the wood with breathing holes at intervals. The female gribble carries about thirty young in a brood pouch and when these hatch out from the mother's brood pouch they tunnel at right angles to the parents' burrow so that the wood becomes riddled with their workings. The effects of the gribble's attack, unlike those of the shipworm's activities, are quite obvious from the outside because the wood looks as though it had been gnawed by beavers. Piles that look quite sound above water may be seen to be so eaten away that they are on the verge of collapse below it. In boats the gribble is much easier to deal with than the shipworm. It is exceedingly sensitive to lowered salinity so that all that is necessary is to tow the boat into brackish or fresh water for twenty-four hours. Boat fishermen in Singapore keep their boats in a fresh water creek when not in use in order to preserve them from gribble.

8

THE OPEN SEA

A BUCKET of sea water looks quite barren of life at first glance and you might be excused for thinking that the open sea away from the shore is as void and destitute of life as the water in the bucket seems to be, and that its only inhabitants above the bottom must be the fishes and porpoises. We know, however, that the surface layers of the sea down to several hundred feet and hundreds, even thousands, of miles from any land are teeming with drifting living creatures, most of them microscopic in size. In order to prove this we have only to tow a pillow case in the sea anywhere at any time; when we pull it in, it is coated with green slime. Under the microscope we see that this green slime consists of myriads of tiny plants and animals. It is the plants that give it the green colour for they contain chlorophyll exactly the same as that in the cells of green plants on land. This is the floating, drifting life of the ocean which we call 'plankton'. It bursts into life in the spring and dies down again (but does not disappear) in the autumn. In the spring the sea water blooms, as do also the lakes, ponds and rivers, just as the fields do on land. First comes an outburst of minute one-celled plants, and this is followed by an outburst of tiny animals, hatched out from eggs spawned earlier in the year. The animals browse upon and devour the plants. The plankton, indeed, is really the cornerstone of the great edifice of life in the sea and all living things in the sea ultimately depend on it, including the great fisheries.

The animals of the plankton belong to every phylum and class of invertebrates and to several vertebrate phyla as well. Many animals, including fish, which live on the bottom during their adult lives begin life as larvae drifting in the plankton. It is not surprising, therefore, to find that certain molluscs have taken to

125

the drifting life and spend their days far out in the open sea travel-
ling passively wherever winds and currents may take them. All
these planktonic molluscs are gastropods and there are no bivalves
which are planktonic as adults though many have minute bivalve
larvae which belong temporarily to the plankton.

Let us suppose that our enthusiasm for shell collecting has
persuaded us to venture out in a drifter or other small ship on the
North Sea. Suppose that when our little ship is drifting and not
under way we tow a fine silk or nylon net, or even a pillow case,
over the windward side. The best time to do this is about an hour
after sunset because the plankton moves up and down in the water
with a daily rhythm, rising to the surface during the hours of
darkness and sinking during daylight. After towing for about ten
minutes we bring in our net or pillow case with its inside glittering with pale and evanescent sparks because all the animals in
the plankton are phosphorescent and glow with a bluish light at
night. If we wash the slime from the net or pillow case (or, rather
more crudely, merely scrape it off with a knife) into a jar of clean
sea water we shall be able to watch all the tiny animals for a
while in a state of furious activity. Minute crustacea are darting
hither and thither. Equally minute jellyfish are pulsing about
in the jar like diminutive transparent bells. Long thin arrow
worms, like darts with pin heads, are jerking spasmodically.
There may be a few rather larger, more massive and fleshy creatures flapping around in the jar with what look like wings. Some
of these creatures have shells or some may be naked.

These are, in fact, molluscs known as 'sea butterflies' belonging
to the order Pteropoda, opisthobranch gastropods related to the
sea slugs. They drift in the open ocean in vast clouds, sometimes
so numerous as to impart a dark coloration to the water. They
are more abundant in northern and southern warm temperate
seas than in the tropics but, numerous as they often are in our
seas, their numbers today are nothing to what they must have
been in past geological epochs for large areas of the floor of the
tropical and temperate mid-Atlantic Ocean consist of a fine, impalpable ooze made up of nothing but the remains of the delicate
shells of sea butterflies. These patches of pteropod ooze, as it is

called, occur over the central ridge of the Atlantic Ocean but are not found in either the Pacific or Indian Ocean although living sea butterflies are as numerous in those oceans as in the Atlantic. In northern, but never in southern, temperate seas the sea butterflies often form the food of whalebone whales which sieve them

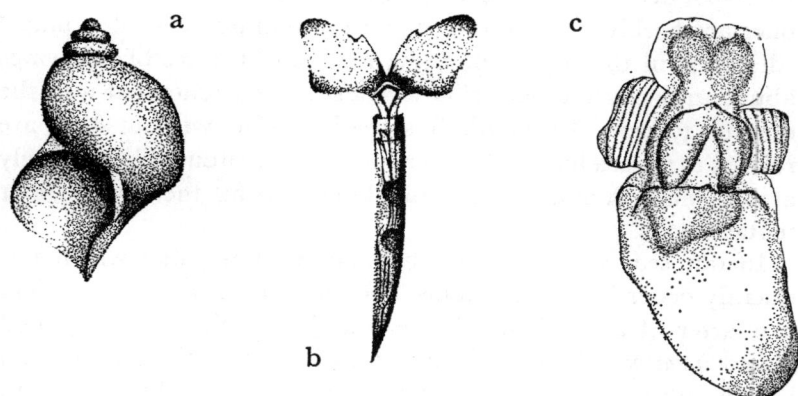

Fig. 33 : Pteropods or Sea Butterflies

With shell A. *Limacina* sp. × 50 approx. B. *Creseis* sp. × 50 approx. With no shell C. *Clione kinkaidi* × 5 nat. size approx.

out of the water by means of the horny plates (baleen) in their mouths.

The sea butterflies (Pteropoda—literally 'wing foot') are so called because of the continuous flapping of their two fleshy wings which keep them afloat. The wings are lateral extensions of the gastropod foot. They flap automatically, but when the water in our jar begins to become deficient in oxygen the animal becomes exhausted and the wings cease flapping. Then it sinks to the bottom like a stone. The sea butterflies have to expend such a lot of energy in order to keep afloat that they are the first in the jar to become exhausted and sink to the bottom.

There are two kinds of sea butterflies, those with shells (Figs. 33a, b) and those without (Fig. 33c). The two kinds are believed to have had a quite separate origin and not to be as closely related as was formerly thought. Those with shells are more abundant in tropical waters than in temperate while those without shells occur equally in both. The shell is very delicate and papery and may be of many different shapes, coiled like that of a snail (*Limacina*), a long, narrow dunce's cap, curved or straight (*Creseis*), a three-pointed shield, vase-shaped and many others. The shelled ones are herbivorous, feeding upon the minute one-celled plants (diatoms) in the plankton. Some have the surfaces of the wings abundantly covered with cilia which set up currents that waft the diatoms towards the mouth. The sea butterflies without shells are related to the sea hare (*Aplysia*) and are carnivorous. They actively attack small animals in the plankton, seizing them with their tentacles.

In our seas we have two common sea butterflies which frequently occur in tow-net hauls, one (*Limacina retroversa*) less than a quarter of an inch in diameter and the other with no shell (*Clione limacina*) like a small slug with wings. Both these are typical inhabitants of Gulf Stream water and they are found in the North Sea only when there is an influx of warm water from the Atlantic Ocean from round the north coast of Scotland. Sometimes they invade the English Channel when warm Atlantic water flows far eastwards towards the Straits of Dover. There are, however, many other species of sea butterflies in our waters some of them with very beautiful shapes, delicate shells and tinted bodies. They are all inhabitants of Atlantic water and to collect them you must usually voyage far off the west coast of Ireland or off the Hebrides. They may be gathered in a silk or nylon tow-net of fine mesh and may be preserved with their wings aspread by putting a few crystals of menthol or chloral hydrate, which are anaesthetics, in the water.

There are other members of the plankton besides these Pteropods which are characteristic inhabitants of water from the Atlantic Ocean; and others, on the other hand, which are typical of the North Sea and English Channel. The presence in the North Sea and English Channel of species characteristic of the Atlantic Ocean is a sign of an influx of warm water from the Atlantic. These influxes are stronger in some years than in others and have

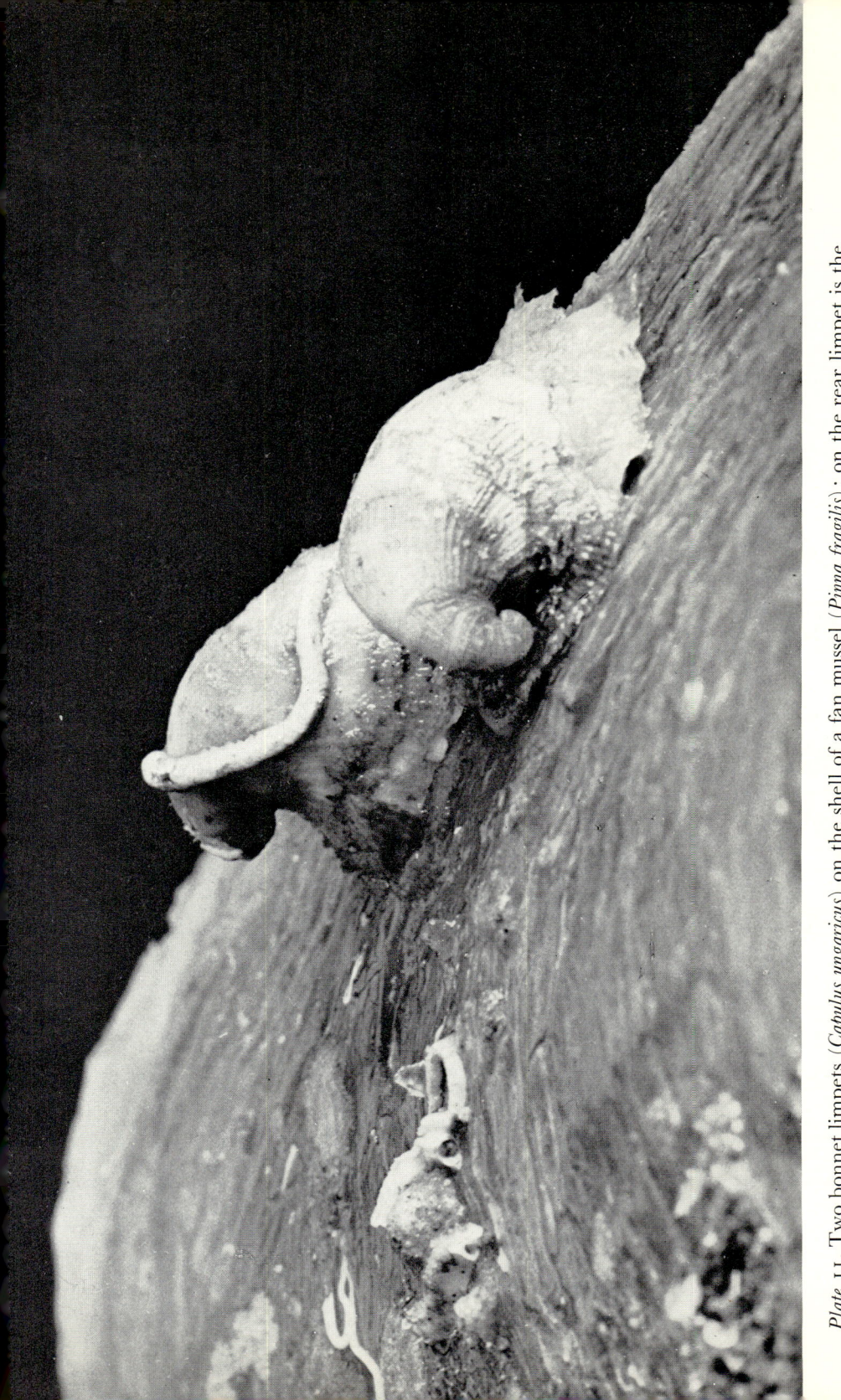

Plate 11. Two bonnet limpets (*Capulus ungaricus*) on the shell of a fan mussel (*Pinna fragilis*) : on the rear limpet is the calcareous tube of a Serpulid worm. *Photo: Douglas P. Wilson, FRPS.*

Plate 12.
A sting
winkle
(*Ocenebra
erinacea*)
feeding on
mussels.
*Photo:
Douglas P.
Wilson, FRPS.*

a profound effect upon the economy of our coastal waters, particularly on the fisheries. They bring pilchards to the coast of
Cornwall and in the North Sea cause diminished catches of
herring. By examining the plankton in their nets in the early
months of the year biologists at Aberdeen and Plymouth can make
forecasts about what the fisheries may expect later in the year.

I am afraid it cannot be said that sea butterflies make very
impressive objects in any collection. Like so many animals of the
plankton they are lovely and enthralling to watch when alive
but drab and uninspiring in death, apt to shrivel up into what
look like little knots of rubber under the influence of the preser-
vative. They are nearly all of minute size, scarcely more than
one-eighth of an inch, although some in the South Atlantic
may reach a quarter of an inch. It is not possible to extract them
from their shells and the whole animal must be preserved in a
glass tube of five per cent formalin. Care must be taken to make
sure that the formalin is quite neutral and not acid since acid
formalin will slowly dissolve away the delicate papery shell (see
p. 47).

In warm seas there are several prosobranch gastropods and one
true snail which have become planktonic and taken to a drifting
life. The prosobranch gastropods belong to the order Heteropoda.
They are found only in tropical waters although isolated specimens are occasionally taken drifting far north in temperate waters.
They are usually found in deep water far from land. One of them
(*Atlanta*—Fig. 34a) has an elongated, transparent body with a
fine, papery but perfectly coiled shell and a small operculum.
The whole appearance is that of a small floating, transparent
snail about two inches long. The whorls of the shell are very flat
and in older animals a characteristic keel runs round the outside
whorl from the first suture to the lip of the aperture. On each side
of the first whorl is a black spot, the eye. The shell is pink or violet
when young but whitish and opaque when older.

Another Heteropod, *Carinaria* (Fig. 34b) has a very thin papery
shell shaped like a republican cap of liberty. The shell is really
dorsal but owing to its relatively heavy weight the animal, which
has an elongated transparent body, lives upside down, carrying

9

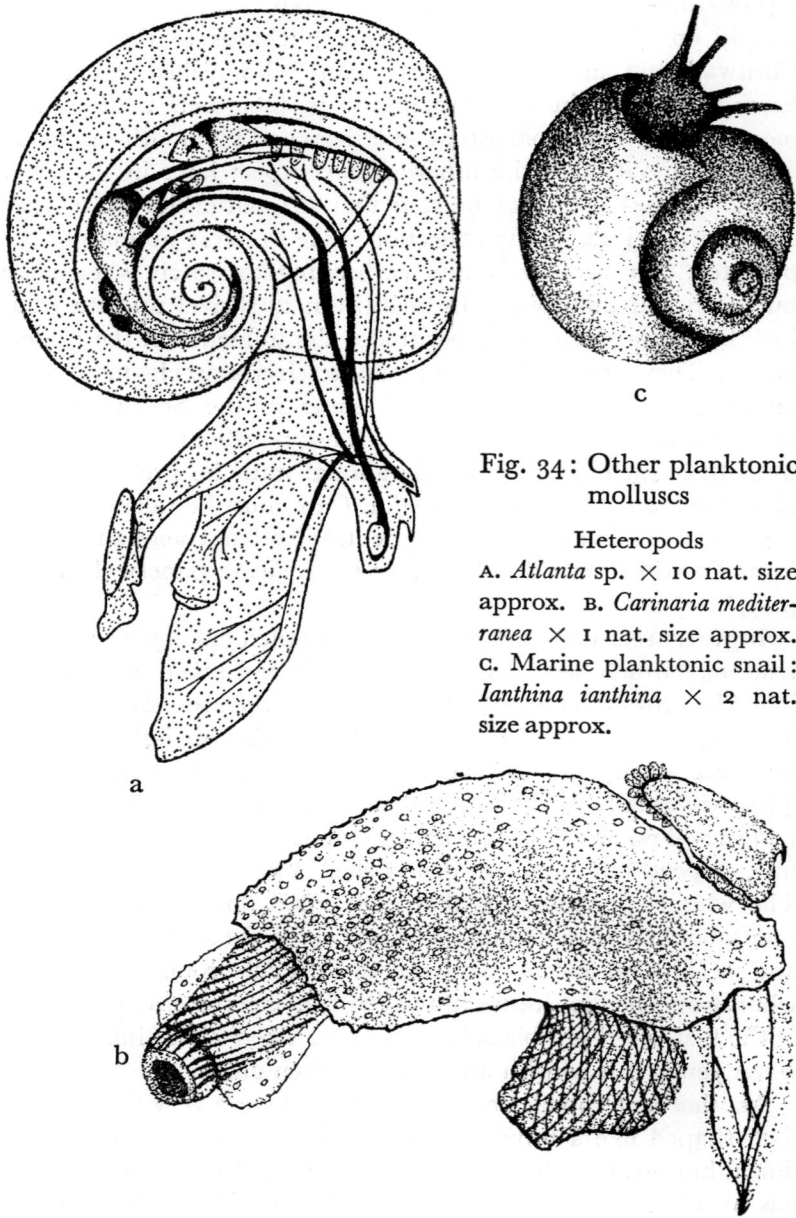

c

a

b

Fig. 34: Other planktonic
molluscs

Heteropods
A. *Atlanta* sp. × 10 nat. size
approx. B. *Carinaria mediter-
ranea* × 1 nat. size approx.
c. Marine planktonic snail:
Ianthina ianthina × 2 nat.
size approx.

the shell downwards. It feeds on jellyfish and small fishes. It must, therefore, be able to move quickly in order to capture its prey, but as a rule when captured it shows few signs of activity at all. *Carinaria lamarcki*, which occasionally drifts into our waters, may reach a length of three inches. A larger species, *C. cristata*, only found in the tropics, has a glassy, transparent, ribbed shell about two inches high, also shaped like a liberty cap. This is sometimes found at sea floating empty and was at one time thought to be the shell of a cephalopod which was called, *in absentia* so to speak, the Glassy Nautilus. It was much prized by collectors in the eighteenth and nineteenth centuries but since it has been discovered to be the shell of a planktonic Heteropod it has quite gone out of fashion. A third genus of Heteropod (*Pterotrachea*) has a single ventral fin under the long transparent body. This is the representative of the foot. There is no shell at all.

Lastly, among the molluscs we must mention an extraordinarily beautiful true snail (*Ianthina*) which is planktonic. It is typically an inhabitant of subtropical waters but quite often drifts as far north as our western coasts and sometimes its delicate blue shells are found cast up on Cornish beaches. It maintains itself afloat by secreting a frothy liquid from a gland in the foot. This at once hardens on contact with the water into an exceedingly tough raft of bubbles which it is impossible to prick with a pin. From this raft the snail hangs upside down floating on the surface of the sea and the shell is therefore dark blue on the first whorl, which floats uppermost, but pale blue on the top of the spire which points downwards. In this it resembles that curious fish, the Nile perch, which, owing to a derangement of the swim bladder, spends its adult life swimming on its back and so in the adult becomes dark on its belly and white on its back and the top of its head. One species (*I. ianthina*—Fig. 34c, Pl. 15), which sometimes visits our waters, produces its young fully formed from inside its body but another (*I. exigua*), which is tropical and is never found as far north as our shores, hangs a row of egg capsules underneath its float. The shell of *I. ianthina* is about three-quarters of an inch in diameter, and the body, which is perfectly snail-like,

with head, tentacles and foot, is about one and a half inches long
when extended.

It was noticed about thirty years ago that visits of *Ianthina* to
our south-western shores always coincided with large numbers
of those floating compound jellyfish known as 'By-the-wind-
sailors' (*Velella*) whose disc-like floats, crowded with individuals
of the colony hanging underneath, skid before the wind over the
surface of the sea propelled by a small vertical sail. Observations
made on board the research ship *Discovery II* have since confirmed
that the *Ianthina* actually feed on the By-the-wind-sailors which
were captured and placed in tanks with the *Ianthina* clinging on
underneath them. In the tanks the *Ianthina* were seen to browse
through the clusters of 'persons' underneath the disc-like float
eventually leaving it quite bare. As they did so the snails from
time to time exuded a dye which was believed to have a paralys-
ing effect on the individuals of the jellyfish colony.

The tiny larvae of many gastropods and bivalves abound in
the plankton especially in inshore waters. The gastropod larva
looks like a very small snail (about one-tenth of an inch in diameter) swimming by means of a ciliated bilobed velum or curtain
by reason of which the gastropod larva is known as a 'veliger' or
curtain bearer. The bivalve larva looks like a diminutive adult
with two transparent yellowish valves through which the organs
of the body and the adductor muscles can be seen as dark smudges.
The larvae of bivalves are about the same size as those of gastropods. In the present state of our knowledge very few of these
larvae, either of gastropods or bivalves, can be certainly related
to an adult form. The larvae of the cowrie, however, are unmistakable for they have a coiled gelatinous, transparent shell dec-
orated with lines of warty protuberances along the spiral of the
whorls. But, again, it is not possible to relate any particular cowrie
larva to any particular adult species.

The molluscs are not the only members of the plankton to have
tests or shells. The vast phylum of the Protozoa, the simplest
single-celled animals, all microscopic and some so small that they
pass through the meshes of the finest nets in use, have external
tests or internal skeletons. These are either made of calcium

carbonate or silica (glass) and show a fantastic variety of shape and pattern. They abound in all seas but especially in warmer latitudes and for many geological ages they have swarmed in the oceans in such numbers that their dead tests and skeletons form deposits of fine ooze covering thousands of square miles of the ocean floor in the greatest depths, far beyond the limits of the finest sediments washed down from the land. An example is the Globigerina whose microscopic calcareous tests make up the floor of vast areas of the tropical oceans and, lifted above sea level during past geological epochs, compose the chalk formations which we know so well.

9

PEARLS AND GEMS

PEARLS have been loved and valued by mankind, and perhaps still more by womankind, since the earliest times. Pliny wrote that they were 'the richest merchandize of all and the most sovereign commodity throughout the world'. Probably we should seek for the origin of the use of pearls far back among very primitive peoples in tropical climates who bought and sold shells and used them as ornaments. The Romans loved pearls and paid huge prices for them, and one of the objectives of Caesar's expedition to conquer Britain may have been the oyster beds that fringed the coast of Britain in those days.

Nevertheless the manner in which pearls come to be formed within the oyster shell remained a mystery for a long time. The Hindus believed that if a dew-drop fell into an open oyster it was transformed into a pearl by the rays of the sun. Another theory held that pearls had something to do with lightning. In the sixteenth century the view was first put forward that pearls result from the activity of a parasite within the oyster.

The oyster which gives the pearl is not related to the edible one but is a cousin of our wing oyster and is therefore more closely related to the mussels. The true pearl oyster (*Pinctada margaritifera*—Fig. 27f), known as the black-lip pearl oyster, is about three inches across with a straight dorsal hinge and the lovely nacre which gives the finest pearls in the world. The magnificent golden-lip or pearl button oyster (*Pinctada maxima*) has a flat pearly shell which may be as much as a foot across but the nacre is of less fine quality than that of the black-lip oyster.

The formation of a pearl is simply the reaction of almost any mollusc to the irritation caused by a foreign body introduced between the mantle and the shell. The mollusc lays down layers of nacre from the shell glands of the mantle around the foreign body. The pearl that is formed, therefore, always has the qualities of the nacreous layer or mother-of-pearl of the shell itself, and only the black-lip pearl oyster has nacre of the lustrous texture and sheen which is so much prized in true pearls.

Very many other molluscs, as a matter of fact, both gastropods and bivalves, also produce pearls, albeit of inferior quality. There is a fresh water pearl mussel (*Margaritifera margaritifera*) which forms pearls of various colours from pink, which are the most valuable, to brown or black. Until late in the nineteenth century there were pearl mussel fisheries in several Scottish rivers, notably the Tay, and the Empress Eugénie of France bought a mussel pearl from New Jersey, U.S.A., for the equivalent of £3,500. The common mussel itself produces pearls of not very high quality, and so do the whelk and several other marine snails. The giant clam of the coral reefs (*Tridacna*) produces large white pearls the size of golf balls that look as though they were made of porcelain, and the big tropical queen conch (*Strombus gigas*), whose flesh is often eaten in the West Indies, sometimes produces pink or red pearls. The tropical turbine shells (Turbinidae), the helmet shells (Cassididae) and the abalone or haliotis shell also form pearls, though usually of a bad shape.

The nacre which forms the pearl is laid down around the foreign body, or nucleus, whatever it may be, in successive concentric layers and it is the light interference caused by these layers which gives the pearl its sheen. Between the successive layers of nacre are exceedingly thin concentric layers of horny material, called conchiolin, similar to that which makes up the periostracum.

Grains of sand or other foreign bodies, such as parasites or eggs, even those of the oyster itself, or the decaying remains of plants or animals, if introduced between the mantle and the shell of the oyster, will normally produce blister pearls. These grow attached to the parent nacreous layer by a small stalk which has to be sawn through in order to get the pearl free. Blister pearls are usually used for making cheap jewellery. Parasites may similarly become enclosed in blisters of nacre. For instance, the North American pearl fish (*Carapus*) regularly lives as a parasite in pearl oysters, but occasionally the host oyster objects and entombs its uninvited guest for ever in a fish-shaped blister of nacre. For centuries the Chinese have had the custom of inserting between the mantle and the shell of the pearl oyster small metal images of Buddha which in due course become covered with mother-of-pearl.

In the pearl fishery of Ceylon true pearls are formed by a parasite, the early stages of the life cycle of a tapeworm. The adult worm lives in the intestine of a large ray which feeds on the oysters. The ray excretes the eggs of the tapeworm into the sea and those which find a temporary home in a pearl oyster complete the first stage of their life cycle there. But sometimes, again, the oyster becomes irritated by its guest and entombs it in a pearl.

A true pearl, as opposed to a blister, must be formed actually within the tissue of the mantle itself. Only in this position can the nacre be laid down equally all round so as to produce a smooth sphere. The best and most perfectly formed pearls come from near the centre of the mantle where they may be pure white, tinted with yellow or flushed with pink. Those formed near the mantle margin are called hem pearls and may be brown or black.

A pearl consists of about 92 per cent calcium carbonate, like the shell of the oyster itself, 4 to 5 per cent of conchiolin and 4 per cent water. The water may evaporate out as the years go by and then the pearl loses its lustre and may become cracked. Since they are made up of such a high proportion of limy substance pearls dissolve in acid, but the process is very slow because the layers of conchiolin give protection to the inner layers of nacre, so that the pearl which Cleopatra dissolved in her wine would have taken several days to disappear. Nevertheless the acids of the human skin do cause slow deterioration after about fifty years, though some fine pearls still exist which are known to be several hundred years old but they have probably not been in regular use.

The pearl oyster or its relations grow in nearly all the warm waters of the world, but the most famous pearl fisheries of all are those of the Red Sea, Persian Gulf and the coast of Ceylon. In the Persian Gulf the pearl fisheries are mostly in the Gulf of Bahrein north of Qatar, between there and Kuwait. In the Red Sea they are mostly on the Sudanese side though there are some pearl oyster beds on the eastern side also. Those on the Sudanese coast of the Red Sea have been known and worked since Roman times and probably long before that. In 300 B.C. Theophrastus wrote: 'Pearls originate in an oyster shell in the Indian and Red Sea.' And Nearchus: 'In the Red Sea lies an island where precious pearls are found. The pearl fishers go into the sea supplied with nets and describe there a great circle. In these nets they enclose the oysters.' This sounds an improbable way of fishing for pearls and it seems probable that the historian was writing about seine-net fishing.

On the Persian Gulf and Red Sea beds live the black lip pearl oyster and its enormous cousin the golden lip or mother-of-pearl oyster which may be a foot across and weigh as much as 12 lbs. The latter gives a rather less lustrous pearl than the former but its splendid flat expanse of nacre is used for pearl buttons (rather less so now since the introduction of plastics) and for mother-of-pearl inlays. The beds were once close to the coast but with continued exploitation they have gradually moved offshore and are now as much as a hundred miles out to sea.

The pearl fishing boats are manned by about ten men each but only two or three of the crew are divers, who are employed by the boat owners. They dive with nothing but a net bag round their necks to put the oysters in, and leather sheaths on their feet and hands to protect them from the jagged coral surfaces. Nowadays some of them use an oxygen apparatus but the majority still go down with only a nose clip in the ancient manner, carrying a heavy stone attached to a line from the surface, with a second line around the waist by which the diver can be hauled up quickly. The average duration of a dive is one and a half minutes and an exceptional dive lasts four minutes. When the oysters are brought up to the surface they may be swiftly opened with a knife to see if there is a pearl inside. Less than one oyster in a hundred has a pearl in it so that this is one of the most wasteful natural resources industries in the world. In boats owned by proprietors, who do not themselves go to sea but merely employ the divers, none of the shells may be opened on board but must be brought ashore and opened under the supervision of the boss. Now that oil has brought such enormous wealth to the Arab states of the Persian Gulf fishing for pearls has undergone a decline. The Arab fishermen find it much more profitable, and much easier and more comfortable, to earn their living from the oil companies in other and less arduous ways.

The Ceylon pearl oyster beds are mostly in the Gulf of Mannar and stretch as a series of banks of coarse granitic sand for about 145 miles between Negombo and Mannar on the west coast of the island. The banks are each about three miles long and 700 yards wide and lie about five miles from the coast in ten to fifteen fathoms. The oyster of the Ceylon pearl fishery (*Pinctada vulgaris*) is not the same as that of the Persian Gulf but gives an equally fine pearl with a pinkish or yellowish tinge. The Ceylon pearl fishery has also declined of recent years largely owing to the growth of the trade in cultured pearls from Japan which now provides the majority of the pearls on the market. But even in its flourishing days before the Second World War it was subject to great and irregular fluctuations owing to the overfishing of the mature oysters, silting up of the beds by the south-west monsoon and devastation by fish such as a big ray which eats the oysters. The fishery was strictly controlled by the government and diving was only allowed when inspection showed that there were enough oysters on the beds. Several years might elapse without any fishing being allowed at all. If inspection by the government inspector showed that there were enough oysters on the beds to make a fishery worth while, an announcement appeared in the local paper that a pearl fishery was to open on such and such a date. Then the little town of Maruchchukaddi, which was the centre of the pearl fishery, enjoyed a temporary boom as the pearl fishermen invaded the town, and temporary quarters, shops and offices were hastily built to accommodate them.

Elsewhere in the east pearls are fished off the Philippines, Celebes, and New Guinea. The oyster is mostly the Ceylon species and in Celebes red, yellow, brown, and black pearls come from a fan mussel (*Pinna nigra*). In Japanese waters the pearl comes from yet another oyster (*Pinctada martensi*) rather smaller than the Ceylon one. It gives white, yellowish or soft pink pearls with a fine lustre. Until recently there was a prosperous pearl fishery off the northern coast of Australia, especially around Thursday Island, but of recent years it has greatly declined. Australian pearls are mostly white and not so iridescent as those of the Persian Gulf or Ceylon and are therefore a good deal less valuable. In the warmer waters of Central America pearl fishing takes place in the Gulf of California, around La Paz, and along the coasts of Nicaragua, Panama and Columbia. Here the pearls come from yet another oyster (*Avicula squamata*) which has a very thin shell. They are light yellow or silver grey. In general pearls from American fisheries, the so-called occidental pearls, are of large size but not of such fine lustre or colour as the oriental ones. They are often irregularly shaped and of various colours, grey, brown, pinkish, greenish or black.

Many attempts have been made to cultivate the black lip pearl oyster and grow it artificially but none with any success until the end of the First World War when an Englishman, Cyril Crosland, working for the government of the (then) Anglo-Egyptian Sudan, succeeded in rearing them at a place called Donganap Bay on the Sudanese coast of the Red Sea. This is a shallow bay of clear water almost totally enclosed by old coral reefs. Here an annual crop of 300 tons of pearl shell was produced in 1922 as compared with a total production for the whole of the Red Sea of 150 tons. Unfortunately in that year the government closed down the experiments which would undoubtedly have had very profitable results if they had been continued. It is good to know that they have now started again under the supervision of the Food and Agriculture Organization of the United Nations. There are now (1966) over a thousand oysters of various ages living on the beds at Donganap Bay and the target production is at present 100 tons of pearl shell per year.

The culture of pearls in oysters has been brought to perfection in Japan where it is now a major industry. The great majority of pearls sold on the market nowadays are cultured pearls from Japan and this has brought about a decline in the pearl oyster fisheries everywhere in the world. At the beginning of the present

century the Japanese pearl oyster beds were devastated by what
is known as a 'red tide'—a sudden proliferation in the water of
immense clouds of one-celled animalcules (Protozoa). These
'red tides' are common enough in the tropics and usually follow
periods of very hot windless weather when, owing to heating of
the surface layers, convection movements—rising of warmed and
sinking of cooled water—cease, so that phosphate salts accumulate
in excessive quantities at the surface. As a result of this, shoaling
fishes and plankton animals die in vast numbers and the sea takes
on a reddish, or sometimes brownish or yellowish, hue by reason
of the clouds of proliferating microscopic organisms. In 1957 a
Russian research vessel cruising in the western Indian Ocean
reported millions of dead fishes over an area of 80,000 square
miles between East Africa and India. Red tides are not uncommon
along the tourist coasts of Florida and have caused much alarm
and inconvenience to holiday makers. Until recently it was believed that the death of these multitudes of fishes and plankton
animals must be due to clogging of the gills or other breathing
organs by the protozoa. In the case of the pearl oyster it was
thought that the gill lamellae became choked so that the oyster
suffocated. Nowadays it is believed that the protozoa actually
give off a poisonous substance which contaminates the water.

In the nineties of the last century an association of Japanese
oyster growers, headed by Kokichi Mikimoto, had already begun
experiments in the rearing of Japanese pearl oysters in the Bay
of Ago, on the southern coast of Honshu Island, Japan. For years
they had also been experimenting by introducing a great variety
of foreign bodies into the oysters in an attempt to induce pearl
formation. Fragments of silver, glass, steel and some types of shell
all produced a reaction. Finally they found that the only thing
that produced the desired response and was not rejected by the
oyster was a small piece of calcareous shell material wrapped in
a tiny bag or sandwich made from the living mantle tissue of the
oyster itself which was to be used for culturing. Curiously enough
the shell material most commonly used nowadays comes from a
North American fresh water clam specially imported into Japan
for the purpose from the shores of the Mississippi. The oysters

with these inclusions are put back in the sea and produce pearls within five to seven years, but in some cases more than one parent oyster may be necessary.

The culture of pearls in Japan was given a great stimulus when the oyster beds failed at the beginning of this century and Mikimoto pearls made by this method are now world famous.

Cultured pearls are every bit as good as real ones and are not in any sense artificial. Nevertheless the price of a real pearl is about ten times that of a cultured one which may be indistinguishable from it in size and quality. It is the price that is artificial, based on intangibles such as snob value, and not the pearl itself. Real and cultured pearls can only be distinguished from one another by special means. X-ray examination reveals the presence of the large nucleus—the introduced foreign body—of the cultured pearl. Examination by fluorescent light reveals the absence of the layers of conchiolin between the layers of nacre in the cultured pearl and their presence in the true pearl. Direct examination of the centre also shows the large nucleus of the cultured pearl but, of course, involves slicing the pearl in half. Cultured pearls react to a magnetic field while true pearls do not.

In Japan pearl diving has always been by tradition a woman's trade. The women dive not only for oysters but for other sea products such as edible seaweeds, urchins and abalones. They are known as *amas* and begin their trade at the age of ten or twelve. The profession is a very closed one, handed down from mother to daughter for generations. Unlike the naked Arab and Ceylonese divers, the Japanese women go down heavily swathed in coarse cotton clothes round their bodies, heads and legs as a protection against attack by sharks and Moray eels. The women are either *kachido* or *funado*. *Kachido* are lone divers who work with a wooden tub floating at the surface to receive what they bring up and to mark their position. *Funado* are husband and wife, and work from a boat, the wife diving and the man working the boat. The women dive to a depth of 20 to 25 feet and stay down for an average of 30 to 40 seconds at each dive. The men never dive; it is considered that women are better divers than men because their bodies are better insulated with fat.

Pearls that are truly artificial are made by coating glass beads with a white substance, called pearl essence, prepared from the belly scales of herrings and sardines. The whiteness of the belly scales of any fish is due to a crystalline substance known as guanin, but only in the herring and sardine and certain small fresh water fishes in France does it have the necessary lustrous quality caused by the formation of minute crystals which break up the light waves and cause interference or iridescence. These artificial pearls are made with either hollow or solid glass beads. The hollow ones are coated on the inside with a mixture of pearl essence and gelatin and the cavity is then filled with wax. The solid ones are coated with pearl essence mixed with celluloid. Hollow bead imitation pearls betray themselves instantly by the reflection from the glass surface, and are much lighter than true or cultured pearls. The solid ones are more durable and more difficult to detect but the celluloid coating can be scraped or burnt off or dissolved off in amyl-acetate. Around the hole through which the string passes the coating of pearl essence and celluloid is irregular while the hole of a true or cultured pearl has quite obviously been drilled.

Less exalted jewellery than pearls is made from many different sorts of shells. Cameo ornaments, usually brooches, so popular in Victorian times, were, and still are, made in Italy from the big helmet shells (Cassididae). These are specially imported into Italy from the Indian Ocean and the two species most often used are *Cassis rufa* and *C. cameo*. The coloured background of the cameo is made of the reverse, outer side of the innermost or nacreous layer of the shell and its colour depends on what species is used. In *C. rufa* it is red. The central white, raised and carved part of the cameo is made of the calcareous layer of the shell which is first polished and then carved after an oval area of red inner layer has been exposed around it by scraping.

During the Victorian craze for shell ornaments and shell jewellery in England, flowers were modelled using small bivalves for petals arranged in intricate designs. There is a charming example in the Natural History Museum, South Kensington, a flower spray with petals made from the small white valves of *Nucula*, the nut shell, so common offshore in the North Sea. There is also a very pretty bracelet made from the bright green cowrie (*Cypraea helvela*) which lives in the Indian and Pacific Oceans. There are also examples of necklaces and bracelets made from various minute marine shells from the South Sea Islands and west coast of North America where the women use shells as ornaments. The sacred Indian chank shell (*Xancus pyrum*), which is taken mostly in the Gulf of Mannar between southern India and Ceylon, has also often been used for making large bangles for the ladies of Bengal, Assam and Behar.

The sacred chank is a heavy, cream-coloured snail about six inches long and it is sacred among Hindus. Legend has it that during the great flood, which figures in so many religious legends, the sacred writings were stolen by an evil spirit and hidden in a chank shell. Vishnu, the Preserver, who is the incarnation of the Supreme Being and manifests himself in many ways, took the form of a fish. He recovered the sacred writings and brought back the chank shell. It stands prominently in many Hindu temples dedicated to Vishnu. Sinistral specimens of the chank are quite common and are especially venerated, mounted in gold and placed in especially prominent positions.

The cowrie shell, because of its shape and appearance, was believed by many primitive peoples to confer fertility on women and at weddings was worn as part of the bridal costume or else presented as an offering. Since the days of ancient Egypt the cowrie has been regarded as an emblem of good luck.

Before mankind took to using discs of metal as a medium of exchange, or money, shells were widely used. The money cowrie (*Cypraea moneta*) was used in many parts of the world but especially by primitive African tribes, the larger shells being used to denote a higher value than the smaller ones. They were still in use in parts of Africa at the end of the nineteenth century. The first metal coins began to be used by the Chinese in 600 B.C. and were cowrie-shaped. The ancient Egyptians also used cowries for money until the arrival of the Greeks who introduced metal discs. The money cowrie, whose natural homes are the Indian and Pacific Oceans, has been found by archaeologists in graves as burial money all over the world, in Scandinavia in the north, in all parts of Africa, India and China and in Indian graves in North America.

The early settlers in America found the Indians using shells as money. They called shell money 'wampun' and it was of two kinds, the black and the white. Black 'wampun' consisted of cylindrical beads carved from the purple portion of the shell of the quahog (*Venus mercenaria*—see pp. 88–89). White 'wampun' or 'peag' was made from the columella of the American knobbed whelk (*Busycon carica*). It was only half as valuable as black 'wampun'. When the colonists arrived they started to manufacture this money in vast quantities so that serious inflation came about and in 1662 it ceased to be legal tender in the New England colonies. The Indian tribes of the western American seaboard used tusk shells (*Dentalium*) as money. Strings of perfect shells were known as 'hiqua' money and were worth forty times the value of broken shells which were known as 'kop-kop'. Tusk shells were still in use as money as late as 1860 in the western states. Farther south the purple shells of a small marine snail, *Olivella*, were used and known as 'kol-kol'.

Plate 13.
The great
scallop
(Pecten
maximus).
Photo:
Douglas P.
Wilson, FRPS.

Plate 14. A white piddock (*Barnea candida*) in its burrow in the peat of a submerged forest on the coast of North Wales. *Photo: Douglas P. Wilson, FRPS.*

10

LIVING TOGETHER

UNDER the conditions of overcrowding and intense competition in which animals live together on the sea shore and in the shallow waters it is inevitable that associations between them, or between animals and plants, should have developed during the course of evolution. Such associations may be quite casual partnerships merely for shelter and protection and may indeed in many cases have started by animals making use of each other's shells, nests, burrows or houses for their own protection. From this we may find the two animals, or an animal and a plant, living together side by side in the same house. Thence we pass to associations in which one partner, or both, may derive some definite benefit from being together. Finally we come to true parasitism where one member of the association lives at the expense of the other.

These associations are found in all the invertebrate classes and among fishes, and it is not surprising that there are several examples among molluscs. In the molluscs it all usually starts by some animal making use of the mollusc's hospitable shell as, for example, the hermit crab does. It uses first the periwinkle shell, then the top and then the whelk shell as it grows older and bigger. Certain small gobies on the eastern coast of the United States take shelter in empty oyster or snail shells, but sometimes one of them is found living in a shell with the oyster or snail still in it apparently quite undisturbed. In the Bahamas there is a little cardinal fish which lives in the mantle cavity at the entrance to a big live sea snail or conch shell, leaving it at night in order to forage for food and then returning to the same shell as to a home. These are the most casual kinds of association in which one partner merely takes shelter with the other without, apparently, giving anything in return.

The case of the carrier shell (*Xenophora trochiformis*) is remarkable in that it is the mollusc which actively seeks out other shells for itself and uses them for its protection. It is a small top shell which glues other empty shells to itself, using single valves of bivalves, by means of a secretion of the mantle margin. Surrounded thus by a cluster of other shells the snail increases the apparent size of its own shell and gains both concealment and protection, thus making it considerably less easy for enemies such as fishes or crabs to seize and devour it.

From the habit of merely taking shelter a more intimate sort of relationship may develop which involves actually sharing the same food. This is called 'commensalism', which means 'eating at the same table'. We have some examples of this on our own shores. One example is the coin shell (*Lepton squamosum*) which lives in the burrows of a soft-bodied prawn. Below low tide mark all around our coasts in sandy mud the soft-bodied burrowing prawns *Upogebia stellata* and *U. deltaura* live in pairs in burrows beneath the sand, each burrow having several entrances. The prawns perpetually fan a current of sea water through their burrows by means of their abdominal legs and feed on the organic particles thus conveyed to them. Because of their inactive existence beneath the sand they have no eyes, their bodies are quite soft and their hinder legs greatly reduced, having indeed no other function than that of fanning a feeding current through the burrow. Inside the burrow with them, and never anywhere else, lives the small white coin shell, a bivalve with an almost square, very thin shell about half an inch long with fine concentric and radiating lines and the entire shell surface punctured by minute pits. The mantle overlaps the margins of the valves and is fringed with long white tentacles. The coin shell is a suspension feeder and benefits from the refuse-bearing current which the prawns constantly waft through the burrow for themselves. It seems unlikely that the prawns get anything at all out of this association and are probably unaware of the lodger within their burrow. The coin shell is rather rare but there are several other much commoner small bivalves which belong to the same family and burrow in sand in the sublittoral zone but do not live in any association.

The montagu shells, named after Colonel Montagu who discovered them, live in association with sea urchins, brittle stars
and sea cucumbers and are much more common than the coin
shell. One of them, *Montacuta substriata* (Fig. 35), is a yellowish
white shell about one-eighth of an inch long which lives attached
by byssal threads to the spines around the anus of the burrowing

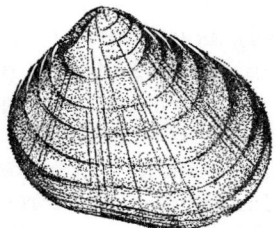

Fig. 35 : Montagu shell: *Montacuta substriata* × 15 nat. size approx.

heart urchin (*Spatangus purpureus*). The urchin burrows in coarse
sand and in the course of its feeding process swallows relatively
enormous quantities of it, extracting the organic matter. One
must presume that the extraction process is not very efficient and
the bivalve lives on the organic matter in the urchin's waste outflow. A second montagu shell (*M. ferruginosa*) is a small reddish
shell about one-third of an inch long living in association with
another burrowing urchin, *Echinocardium cordatum*. It lives attached
to the wall of the urchin's burrow opposite the anus and benefits
from the urchin's excretory products in the same way as *M. substriata*.

None of these small bivalves is ever found away from its partner
or living in partnership with any other species, not even a related
one. The associations do not seem to benefit the molluscs' larger
partners in the least—they simply share the same food. In the
much closer and more intimate relationships known as 'symbiosis',
or 'living together', the two partners have become mutually
dependent, and one, sometimes both, cannot live except in association with the other. One of the strangest examples of this intimate
type of association was studied by scientists* of the Great Barrier

* C. M. Yonge, 1936. *Sci. Rep. Gt. Barrier Reef Exped. 1928–9*, 1, No. 11. pp. 213–
321, London.

Reef Expedition, 1928–29. It occurs in the giant clam (*Tridacna*) of tropical coral reefs. There are four species of giant clam which either burrow or just lie on the surface of the reef in shallow water, hinge downwards with their huge crenellated valves agape. One of them, *Tridacna gigas*, is the largest mollusc known and may reach a length of four and a half feet and a width of two and a half feet, weighing four hundredweight, a fifth of a ton. The sheer weight of these giant bivalves is enough to keep them firmly anchored in position on the reef so that corals and other growths and weeds grow up around them until nothing can be seen but the gaping slit lined by the soft, brightly coloured mantle edge. But if some unwary human being should accidentally put an arm or leg into the slit the huge valves close instantly and no force can open them. This has actually happened to fishermen on the Great Barrier Reef and the unfortunate victim, held by the arm or leg in a vice-like grip, has been drowned by the incoming tide. Since these bivalves maintain themselves in position by weight alone they have no foot and no byssus and the two valves do not gape when closed.

Two other species (*Tridacna crocea* and *Hippopus hippopus*) do not run to such an enormous size. They actually burrow into the substance of the coral rock until they are enclosed in it up to the edges of the valves. These clams do have a foot by means of which they explore the coral rock looking for a place free from coral polyps where they can begin to burrow. This they do by attaching themselves by a byssus and rocking backwards and forwards so that their sharply ridged shells grind away the soft coral rock. The hinge side of the valves does the grinding so that the shell subsides into the coral rock margin upwards.

All these clams, both burrowing and non-burrowing, have undergone an internal contortion so that the foot and byssus, where they exist, come out on the hinge side of the shell which gapes widely to make way for them. The inhalent and exhalent siphons are apertures between the mantle lobes that fringe the free edges of the shell. The inhalent siphon has the form of a slit between the fleshy mantle lobes while the exhalent siphon has a short projecting spout (Pl. 16).

These huge shells are dotted about the reefs in great numbers, agape in the clear, warm shallow water. The soft, fleshy, brilliantly coloured mantle margins overlap the wavy edges of the shell like a lobed skirt and in many cases nothing can be seen of the clam itself. The fleshy mantle lobes of the biggest clam (*Tridacna gigas*) are brown and olive green with emerald green spots. Those of the burrowing one (*T. crocea*), which is quite common on the reefs around Singapore, are bright blue with green flecks. In the middle of each fleshy skirt can be seen the slit of the inhalent siphon and the spout of the exhalent one. From time to time each shell feels the need to clear itself of sand which it does by suddenly clapping its valves together, sending up a spout of water into the air from the exhalent siphon. These jets of water can be seen spouting into the bright sunshine on every hand.

But the most remarkable feature of these giant clams is to be found in their mantle lobes. On close examination the surface of the lobes can be seen to be covered with multitudes of minute specks of some clear, colourless material. These are called the 'hyaline' (clear) organs. Along the outer surfaces of the mantle lobes the hyaline organs are disposed in rows and lie flush with the surface of the mantle tissue. Towards the gape of the shell, away from the shell margins, the hyaline organs are raised up on the top of papillae or tubercles which become higher and larger towards the apposed lips of the mantle edges in the midline of the gape of the shell (Pl. 16).

Microscopical examination shows that the tissues of the fleshy mantle lobes are in fact crowded with single-celled plants which live within the tissues and are actually carried about in the bivalve's blood. These are called Zooxanthellae and are perfectly genuine plants living a plant-like life of their own in the mollusc's tissues, photosynthesizing the sunlight to form carbohydrates from carbon dioxide and water as do all green plants everywhere. They live not only in the tissues of the mantle lobes of the clam, though they are most abundant there, but are also found in the internal organs of the body. They crowd chiefly into the mantle lobes because they need sunlight in order to carry out their life processes and the clam keeps its mantle lobes exposed to the bright sunlight all day long partly with the object of encouraging their growth. It used to be thought that the clear specks, the hyaline organs, on the mantle lobes were light perceiving organs of some sort but it has been shown that they are in fact clear crystalline patches which act like lenses to focus and concentrate the sunlight. Since they are foci for sunlight the zooxanthellae proliferate in the tissues beneath and around them by simple division until the tissues under the hyaline organs become engorged with zooxanthellae. Thus it comes about that the older hyaline organs, nearest the gape and farthest from the shell margin, become raised up on tubercles whose sole function is to act as reservoirs for the plant cells.

Periodically, when it feels the need, the clam devours its own zooxanthellae in enormous numbers. This it does by means of special devouring cells, called phagocytes—literally 'eating cells' —which it carries in its blood stream. These migrate towards the plant reservoirs, the tubercles under the hyaline organs, engulf the plant cells, carry them away in the blood stream and dissolve them. Thus the giant clam actually farms the zooxanthellae in its tissue and uses them as a form of food. It has developed the hyaline organs in order to concentrate the sunlight and encourage them and it is for this purpose too that the clam lies all day agape with its mantle edges exposed to the full rays of the tropical sun. Here, then, is an association for mutual benefit, a symbiosis, since the plants are housed, provided with sunlight and fed by the bloodstream of the mollusc which, for its part, has a supply of food ready to hand whenever it needs it. But while the zooxanthellae cannot live outside the mollusc, the mollusc can, and sometimes does, live without the zooxanthellae.

Associations such as this between invertebrate animals and single-celled plants are not uncommon in the marine world. All coral polyps, for instance, live in symbiosis with zooxanthellae much as the giant clam does. The plants live in the polyps' tissues, especially around the mouth and tentacles, and are in many cases numerous enough to give the polyps a green colour. If food becomes short the polyp extrudes the zooxanthellae from its tissues into its stomach cavity and ingests them. In some corals the polyps are entirely dependent on the zooxanthellae which fill the whole stomach cavity so that the polyp cannot feed in the ordinary way at all and so cannot live without them. It is because of the necessary, and in some cases vital, presence of these plant cells in their tissues that corals must always live in clear, shallow water brightly lit by the sun. Like the giant clams they encourage the growth of their plant partners by doing so.

Many sponges, hydroids, anemones and flatworms also live in association with green plants which inhabit their tissues. The best known case of such symbiosis on the sea shore is that of the small flatworm, *Convoluta*, which lives on sandy shores on the Brittany coast and looks like smears of some green slime trailing from the rocks down towards the sea. Its brilliant green colour is due to the presence in its tissues of zooxanthellae beneath the skin of the small flatworm. The worm starts life with a mouth and alimentary canal, able to feed in the ordinary way on organic particles in the sand. In due course it finds it easier to live on the starch produced by the photosynthesis of its plant cells so that the mouth and alimentary canal degenerate and disappear. In order to encourage their plant cells the little flatworms rise to the surface of the sand in great numbers when the tide goes out and then appear as green smears. They sink beneath the surface of the sand again when the tide returns.

11

FOSSIL SHELLS

FOSSILS are the relics or traces of living creatures preserved in the rocks of the earth's crust. They occur only in sedimentary rocks laid down in water usually, though not always, in shallow seas. Such rocks may result from the break-down and redisposition of older, earlier formed rocks or they may result from the deposition of dead animal or plant remains. Grits, sandstones, clays and shales are formed from the break-down of rocks already in position and then eroded by wind, wave and water. Chalk, various kinds of limestone and coal result from the death and decay of animal or plant remains. Other sediments may result, like our own oolitic limestone which covers so much of the midlands of England, from the consolidation around minute nuclei of calcium carbonate precipitated out of sea water.

Only the hard parts of animals or plants can form fossils because the soft parts, as one might expect, decay away. But deposits of sediment raining down from above, or sudden overwhelmings by banks and shoals of sediments, may bury living creatures so that their hard parts, external or internal skeletons, shells or woody structures, persist long after the soft tissues have decomposed and vanished. Trees and plants fall and accumulate in decay and are buried by the deposit of sediments above them. Slow replacement of organic substances by mineral compounds takes place, molecule by molecule, so that the hard parts of the once living animal or plant remain faithfully modelled in every detail but composed entirely of minerals derived from the enveloping rock. Sometimes the replacement mineral consists of glittering pyrites crystals (iron or copper sulphide) or glowing opal (silica deposited out of solution). Fossils may also be casts or impressions. Casts result when a deposit of sediment fills the inside of a shell or hollow cavity in the once living skeleton. It then retains the exact shape of the cavity long after the hard part has been dissolved away just as a jelly retains the shape of the mould. Impressions are formed around the outside surface of the hard part.

Fossils are found in sedimentary rocks of every age from the very oldest known (pre-Cambrian sandstones and limestones), which are 500 to 600 million years old, up to the newest, the holocene peats and beaches now still in process of formation. It has, therefore, been possible to deduce from fossils a wealth of information about the history and evolution of life on earth. By arranging known fossils in time sequences, noting the slow changes which such sequences reveal as having taken place from the very oldest fossils to the very newest, geologists can trace the progress, rise to dominance and sometimes total extinction of the various races of animals and plants that have populated the earth during the history of life upon it. Many races, it can be seen, evolved into fantastic and gigantic forms, like the giant reptiles of the tertiary era. Some dominated for a while and then vanished, as have the giant reptiles and the great coiled molluscs, the ammonites. Other races have survived unchanged throughout countless centuries and many geological epochs, remaining today, like the commonest of our humble garden weeds, the equisetum or horsetail, almost exactly as they were in remote geological epochs. The horsetail is today identical, though much reduced in size, with its ancestors of the far off times of the coal measures.

The oldest known sedimentary rocks, 500 to 600 million years old, are young compared with the globe itself which is estimated to be 4,500 million years old. Before the first stratified sedimentary rocks were laid down the earth's crust was built up solely of crystalline rocks, many of them cooked and altered by pressure and heat. They formed the cooling crust of the hot spinning globe. Such rocks are the granites, basalts and lavas that we know today. Fossils could never be formed in crystalline rocks because such rocks result from cataclysmic processes involving enormous heat and pressure. They cooled from molten liquids aeons before life appeared on the planet. But sedimentary rocks were laid down by processes of slow deposition or swift smothering which entrapped the living inhabitants. Nor could fossils be formed until the animals or plants had evolved hard external or internal skeletons or woody tissues which could resist decay long enough to become mineralized. Life on this planet, therefore, was quite well advanced long before the time indicated by the appearance of the earliest traces of fossils. The oldest undoubted fossils have been found in rocks known to be between 450 and 500 million years old, though obscure traces of what might have been living creatures have been detected in rocks known to be between 500 and 600 million years old. Before that, over a vast stretch of time, all animals were soft-bodied invertebrates and it is believed that we must look for the origins of life itself some 2,700 million years ago.

The sedimentary rocks laid down during the comparatively short period of 500 million years of our earth's history have been arranged in succession by geologists according to their estimated age. They now stand in a time sequence, graded and labelled, from the oldest to the newest. The stretch of time thus embraced is divided for convenience into three, or sometimes four, great eras, the primary (covering 300 million years), the secondary (covering 150 million years), and the tertiary (covering about 50 million years up to the present day). Sometimes the latest million years of all is chopped off the tertiary era to make a quaternary era during which all the very newest deposits have been laid down. Alternatively these eras may be known respectively as the palaeozoic (ancient life), mesozoic (middle life) and the caenozoic (recent life). Before the palaeozoic, back to the earth's origin, lies a gulf of time known as the azoic (no life) or proterozoic (first life) era.

Each of these three or four eras is again divided into a number of geological periods during which rocks of similar age were laid down in various parts of the world. Each period covered an estimated time space of about 50 million years. These periods provide a fairly accurate time table for the deposition of sediments all over the world. Geologists can recognize and trace sedimentary rocks belonging to the same period, and therefore of the same age, wherever they crop out all over the face of the globe and know, for example, that the London clay, the *calcaire grossier* of central France and the marl clays of New Mexico, U.S.A., are all of the same approximate age, having all been laid down roughly during the same period in the earth's history. Appendix 1 shows a list of the eras and periods into which the geological history of the earth is divided for the convenience of geologists, together with the kinds of rocks which were laid down during each period in Britain.

Molluscs have always been ideal subjects for fossilization. They have a calcareous external hard shell easily dissolved and replaced, and they live in shallow seas or on beaches where the deposition of sediments and the movements of banks and shoals have been going on continuously throughout the history of life on earth. They are, therefore, common as fossils in all the fossil-bearing sedimentary rocks except the very oldest. The molluscs are an extremely ancient race and were already provided with bivalved and coiled shells when they appeared first in rocks of Cambrian age. There were only a few gastropods and bivalves at this time, however, and most of the gastropods had uncoiled shells. There were also some other cornet-shaped shells, very thin and delicate, which may have belonged to planktonic molluscs similar to our modern sea butterflies. A few of these may have been early cephalopods.

From the Cambrian age until they disappeared during the Devonian there lived a fairly abundant race of Monoplacophora. These have reappeared mysteriously during our twentieth century. In fossil form they look very much like limpets and it is probable that many fossils of this age which are thought to be limpets will in fact turn out on re-examination to be Monoplacophora. In well preserved specimens traces of the segmental arrangement of the muscles and gills can be seen (see page 18).

Chitons first appeared in Cambrian times and have continued unchanged to the present day. They are now much more abundant than they have ever been before.

Cephalopods became fairly abundant in the Ordovician period, mostly with slender, straight or curved shells. They were generally not more than a few inches long but one, *Endoceras*, reached a length of fifteen feet. Today the Nautilus is the only surviving cephalopod with an external shell. Some of the large number of cephalopods with external shells which filled the seas of Ordovician times are found as fossils in rocks which were laid down in deep water so that in those days they obviously ranged far from land. Coiled snails became fairly common in the shallower of the seas of these times but bivalves were not yet very abundant. In the Silurian period cephalopods were still more abundant than any other molluscs and there were then as many with coiled or curved as with straight shells.

In Devonian seas tusk shells appeared for the first time and have persisted practically unchanged to the present day. Cephalopods with tightly coiled flat shells, called ammonoids (their fossils being called ammonites) occurred for the first time (Fig. 36a, b). Their shells were divided into chambers separated by walls or septa. As the animal grew it moved forward, as our modern Nautilus does, into the lowest, widest part of its coiled shell and sealed itself off from behind by secreting a wall or septum, except for a central canal called the 'siphuncle', which traversed the whole spiral and ran through each wall and each chamber in turn, again as in the Nautilus. The ammonoids carried an operculum on their bodies which closed the aperture of the shell. In some it resembled that of a modern coiled gastropod but in others it had a double shape and looked like the two valves of a bivalve. As fossils these were often found isolated from the ammonite to which they belonged and were thus mistaken for the fossils of true bivalves. On the outside of the shell of the ammonoid the septa were visible as suture lines which traced a zig-zag course over the shell surface and these can also be seen in fossil ammonites. In the early ammonoids, called Goniatites (Fig. 36a), which lived in Silurian seas, the suture lines were simple zig-zags but they became more elaborate and sinuous in later types. Gastropods and bivalves were still comparatively unimportant during the Silurian period.

Carboniferous rocks were largely laid down under swamp conditions. This was the period when the coal measures were formed in soft, steamy, boggy lakes and estuaries where bivalves became important and abundant for the first time. There were scallops,

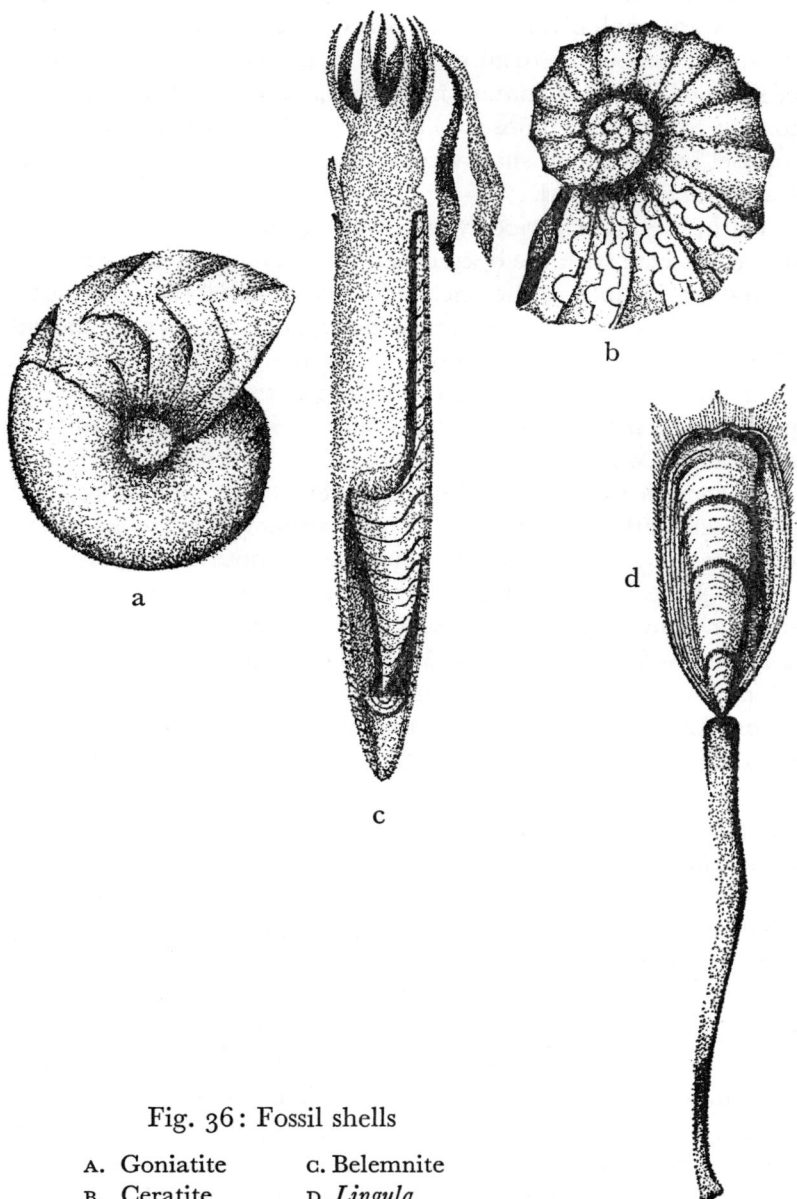

Fig. 36 : Fossil shells

A. Goniatite   c. Belemnite
B. Ceratite   D. *Lingula*

a kind of cockle and several sea snails. There were fan mussels and several small bivalves (*Nuculana*) which resembled our modern nutshells. Among the coal measures in England there are bands of shale which often contain numerous remains of mussels related to our fresh water mussel. These are known to the miners as 'mussel bands'. Land snails occurred for the first time during the Carboniferous period.

In the Permian period, which was a time of shallow enclosed seas connected with the open ocean by channels, bivalves became abundant, mainly in the enclosed seas, while in the open ocean ammonoids were still numerous. Belemnoids, known as 'belemnites' as fossils (Fig. 36c), appeared for the first time. They were cuttle fish with cylindrical, cigar-shaped shells. In the Triassic period, which was really a continuation of Permian conditions, ammonoids were still abundant but they had septa marked by very complicated suture lines with elaborate sinuosities, frills and crenellations (Fig. 36b). These ammonoids are known as Ceratites. Coiled snails were abundant in both these periods.

The Jurassic was a mild period during which the land was sinking, and warm muddy seas were spreading over much of what is now Europe and Asia. It was the heyday of the ammonoids which became exceedingly abundant and dominated the marine fauna. Indeed ammonites are the indicator fossils of the period for they can be used to identify rocks of jurassic age wherever they occur all over the world. Some had smooth and some sculptured shells, some with simple and some with complicated suture lines. Some swam at the surface while others crawled on the sea bottom, and many were of giant size like cart-wheels. Belemnoids were also very abundant, especially in the muddy seas which were characteristic of this period.

The belemnoids were the ancestors of all our modern cephalopods (octopuses, squids and cuttles), but not of the Nautilus which is of much older lineage, descended from the straight and curved forms which were already flourishing in Ordovician seas. The belemnoids had straight but complicated shells (Fig. 36c). The animal itself inhabited the outer section of a front, thin-walled chambered portion of the cylinder. This is called the 'phragmacone' and carries a dorsal forward extension called the 'pro-ostracum'. It fitted into a much stouter and stronger conical portion, called the 'guard', which protected it. In fossil belemnites the 'guard' is known as the 'thunderbolt' or 'bullet' and is often the only part of the animal which survives in the fossil state. It can still be detected today in cuttlefish bones as a tiny apical stalk.

Fresh water snails became very abundant in the Jurassic period and our Purbeck marble, of which the piers of Salisbury cathedral were built, consists largely of their remains.

The Cretaceous was the period of the chalk and the ammonoids were abundant at first but later began to throw off uncoiled, straight, or irregularly shaped forms and by the end of the period they had become extinct. The development of such strange and bizarre shapes always seems to be a sign of approaching demise in any race and it can be observed in many of the once great but now extinct or diminished races of animals, both vertebrate and in-vertebrate. The giant reptiles provide another striking example of this. Belemnoids, too, began to decline in number during the Cretaceous period.

During the following Eocene period a great ocean extended across what are now the Mediterranean, the Himalayas and central Asia. It is known to geologists as the Tethys sea. Inverte-brate life was extremely prolific in it and the molluscs were almost indistinguishable from those of today. There were oysters, cockles, mussels and the shipworm. Gastropods—horn shells (*Cerithium*), cowries (*Cypraea*), and spindle shells (*Fusinus*)—were as abundant then as they are now in tropical seas. Ammonoids and belemnoids had disappeared leaving only the Nautilus and some early cuttle-fish.

Sea shells, therefore, as we now know them, have been with us practically since fifty million years ago when the London clay was laid down. Their ancestors, not very different from them, go back 500 million years to the earliest sedimentary rocks. In the Miocene period, after the Eocene, about twenty million years ago, sea shells became enormously abundant in certain parts of the world, so much so that in some of the warm, shallow lagoons of that period, vast banks of their shells were formed and now remain in, for instance, south-western France as deposits known as *faluns* composed entirely of shells, largely of warm water gastropods such as *Conus*, still common in tropical seas.

So we see that the molluscs, like many other races of animals during the history of life on earth, have had periods of dominance, when they were the most abundant, various and largest animals living in their environment. Such was the Jurassic period when the ammonoids filled the seas and the Miocene when gastropods predominated locally. These in their turn diminished and some, like the ammonoids and belemnoids, became extinct and are only known to us now as fossils. But the molluscs as a race are still with us, a successful and flourishing phylum of the animal kingdom.

The lamp shells (Brachiopoda) have already been mentioned briefly (Chapter 1). They look very much like bivalve molluscs at first glance and inhabit mostly rather deep offshore waters. They are, in fact, not molluscs and bear no relation to them. Their bivalved shells are usually calcareous but may be made of horny material, and they consist of upper and lower, and not right and left, valves. The lamp shells are ciliary feeders and have inside the shell a complicated armature, spiral in some species, which is ciliated and wafts a sea water current through the shell. They are usually anchored to a rock by a stalk but one genus, *Lingula*, common in warm tropical muddy shores, has a horny bivalve shell and burrows by means of a long tubular stalk which functions like a molluscan foot. Our modern lamp shells are the much reduced residue of a once flourishing race which peopled the seas in Ordovician and Silurian times, 350 to 400 million years ago. In Ordovician seas they were the dominant animals and the fossil *Lingula* (Fig. 36d) of those times is identical with the small stalked creature that can today be found burrowing in the mud of Malayan beaches. During the Silurian period lamp shells were so abundant that their calcareous shells formed beaches persisting as shell deposits to this day. They continued in abundance through the Permian period but were then already diminishing. Most of the Silurian forms died out in Permian times while,

Plate 15. Two pelagic snails (*Ianthina ianthina*) floating at the surface of the water by means of their bubble rafts. The specimen on the left is shedding a cloud of ink. *Photo: Douglas P. Wilson, FRPS.*

Plate 16.
A giant clam (*Tridacna gigas*) embedded in coral on the Great Barrier Reef, showing the fleshy mantle lobes between the open valves. The slit-like inhalent siphon can be seen on the left and the spout-like exhalent siphon on the right: the white spots are the 'hyaline' organs. *Photo: M. J. Yonge.*

again, some very elaborate and specialized forms appeared. In the Jurassic and Cretaceous periods the lamp shells continued slowly to decline, while giving off more strange specialized forms, and by the Eocene were reduced to their present residual status as interesting survivors of a once dominant race.

Eras and Periods into which the geological history of the earth is divided				
Age	Duration	Era	Period	Deposits
8,000 B.C.		QUATERNARY	Holocene	Deposits formed since the retreat of the ice, alluvial river deposits, beaches, peats
Millions of Years				
I			Pleistocene	Gravels, boulder clays, ice-dropped deposits, raised beaches
14	15	CAENOZOIC or TERTIARY	Pliocene	Shelly sands, coral sands
20	35		Miocene	Lake and lagoon deposits
15	50		Oligocene	Marls, clays, limestones, sandstones
20			Eocene	Clays, sands
50	70	MESOZOIC or SECONDARY	Cretaceous	Chalk, sands, shales
30	120		Jurassic	Marble, limestones, shales, clays, sandstones
40	150		Triassic	Lias, oolitic limestone, sandstones, clays
30	190	PALAEOZOIC or PRIMARY	Permian	New Red Sandstone, magnesian limestone, marls
60	220		Carboniferous	Coal measures, grits, shales, iron-stones, sandstones, conglomerates
40	280		Devonian	Old Red Sandstone, grits, slates, shales, limestones
30	320		Silurian	Shelly sandstones, coralline limestones, grits, shales, mudstones
50	350		Ordovician	Limestones, sandstones, mudstones, shales, slates
100	400		Cambrian	Slates, flags, coarse sandstones
	500–1,750	AZOIC or PROTEROZOIC	Pre-Cambrian	Sandstones

together with the kinds of rocks laid down during each period in Britain	
Localities	Molluscs as Fossils

Localities	Mono-placophora	Loricata (Chitons)	Gastropods	Bivalves	Modern	Cephalopods	Ammonites	Belemnites	Nautilus	Tusk shells
East Anglia, Cheshire, Salop, Lancs., Scotland										
St. Erth (Cornwall), Norfolk, Suffolk										
None in Britain, *Faluns* in S.W. France										
Bembridge (Isle of Wight), Barton (Hants.)										
Barton (Hants.), Bracklesham (Selsey, Sussex), London clay										
Chalk formations of southern England, Gault and Greensand of Kent, Surrey and Sussex										
Portland stone, Purbeck (Dorset) marble, Lyme Regis (Dorset), Kimmeridge (Dorset) clay, Whitby, Sutherland (Scotland)										
Hebrides, Oxford clay, Langport (Somerset), Westbury (Wilts.), Worksop (Notts.), Cheshire, Durham										
Eden Valley (Cambs.), Isle of Man, Lancs., Cheshire, Durham, Yorks., Notts.										
Tyneside, Lanark, Yorks., Bristol, Forest of Dean, Warwickshire, N. Cornwall, Somerset, Derby, S. Wales										
N. Devon, S. Devon (Torquay), S. Cornwall, Scotland, Welsh borders										
Wenlock and Wrekin (Salop), Llandovery, Rhayader, Haverfordwest (Pembs.)										
Girvan (Ayr), Bala, Cader Idris, Llandeilo, Llanwrtyd, Skiddaw slates (Cumberland)										
Isle of Man, Tremadoc (Wales), S.E. Ireland, Salop, Scotland										
Longmynd (Salop), Torridon (Scotland)										

APPENDIX II

Adductor muscle — The muscle which attaches the animal to the wall of the shell in bivalves and by contraction closes the shell, drawing the two valves together. It may be anterior or posterior or there may be only one (the posterior muscle). The places of attachment of the adductor muscles to the insides of the valves can be seen as scars on the insides of the empty valves.

Aperture — Opening or entrance to the shell in gastropods.

Apex — The part of the shell which is formed first during the life of the animal. In coiled gastropods it is the first whorl of the spiral, in limpets the pointed crown, in bivalves the beak of each valve, in *Chiton* the tip of the crest in the middle line of the dorsal scutes or shields.

Axis — The perpendicular line through the apex about which the shell is coiled in gastropods. The perpendicular to the long axis passing through the beak or umbo in bivalves.

Beak — Or umbo. The curved, often protuberant part of the apex of the valves in bivalves. In *Chiton* the same as the apex.

Byssus — Or beard. The fibrous outgrowth by

means of which many bivalves (e.g. the common mussel) attach themselves.

Callus — The thickened lip of the aperture in gastropods.

Calcareous layer — The middle, crystalline, limy layer of the three layers which compose the shell.

Cancellate (adj.) — Intersecting ribs and ridges.

Cardinal teeth — Central articulating teeth on the hinges of the shells of bivalves.

Carinate (adj.) — Keeled.

Chitinous (adj.) — Made of chitin, the horny substance which composes the external skeleton of the insects and crustacea.

Chondrophore — A spoon-shaped projection, or in some cases a pit, for the attachment of the internal ligament in bivalves, notably in *Mya*.

Cingulate (adj.) — Spirally sculptured or ornamented.

Columella — Literally 'little column'. The central pillar around which the spiral is coiled in coiled gastropods.

Conchology — The science of the study of shells, as opposed to malacology, the science of the study of molluscs.

Convolute (adj.) — Term applied to the condition where the last or outer whorl of a coiled gastropod conceals the inner one so that no umbilicus (q.v.) is present. See involute.

Costa/costae — Rib/s.

Crenulate (adj.) — Having a notched edge.

Ctenidium/ctenidia — Comb-like gill/s.

Decollate (vb.) — To discard the apical whorls.

Dextral (adj.) — Right handed coiled gastropod. The spiral winds clockwise from the apex

	to the aperture which is on the right hand of the spire (see sinistral).
Dimyarian (adj.)	Having two adductor muscles, anterior and posterior.
Epidermis	The outer layer of skin. This term is sometimes wrongly applied to the brown outer layer or periostracum of the shell.
Equilateral (adj.)	Opposite sides the same. Applied to bivalves when the valves are the same shape and size both fore and aft of the umbo. Converse—inequilateral.
Equivalve (adj.)	Applied to bivalves when both valves are the same shape and size—mirror images of one another. Converse—inequivalve.
Foot	The muscular base of the body of a mollusc, usually protrusible from the shell and used for locomotion. In cephalopods much modified into a crown of tentacles.
Front end	Of bivalves. In order to tell the front from the rear end of a bivalve hold the shell hinge uppermost with the beaks pointing forward. The ligament is behind them and the lunule (q.v.) in front of them. The siphons and pallial sinus (q.v.) are at the rear.
Gape	The space between the valve margins, usually accommodating the siphons, when the shell is quite closed.
Gills	Breathing apparatus. May be comb-like or curtain-like or part of the mantle.
Gill chamber	Cavity or chamber in which the gills are situated, usually the same as the mantle cavity (q.v.).

Girdle	Of chitons. The muscular, flexible, oval ring around the central plates.
Growth line/s	The lines on the outside of the shell which mark pauses in growth during the life of the mollusc, concentric in bivalves and limpets, vertical in coiled shells.
Hinge	The dorsal line along which the valves of bivalves meet and articulate.
Holostomatous (adj.)	Literally 'entire mouthed'. Of gastropods. The lip of the aperture has no notch, groove, or canal for a siphon.
Imperforate (adj.)	Without an umbilicus (q.v.).
Inner lip	Inner margin of the aperture of gastropods from the base of the columella to the suture (q.v.). Often thickened.
Involute (adj.)	Term applied to the condition where the last or outer whorl of a coiled gastropod conceals the inner one but an umbilicus (q.v.) is present. See convolute.
Lateral teeth	Subsidiary articulating teeth on either side of the central cardinal teeth of bivalves. See cardinal teeth.
Left valve	Applied to bivalves. The valve on the left of the mid-dorsal line.
Ligament	The elastic fibrous band between the valves of a bivalve the contraction of which causes the valves to separate. It lies posterior to the beaks or umbos (q.v.).
Lip	The margin of the aperture of a gastropod, often thickened.
Lunule	A heart-shaped or triangular depression in the mid-dorsal line of bivalves immediately in front of the beaks or umbos.

Malacology	The science of the study of molluscs (as opposed to conchology, the science of the study of shells).
Mantle	Or pallium. A fold of the skin of the body of a mollusc arising originally on each side of the mid-dorsal line and enveloping the body in part or wholly, like a cloak. It becomes much modified, secretes the shell, may bear sensory organs along its margin or be drawn out so as to form tubes or siphons.
Mantle cavity	The cavity or space between the body of the animal and the mantle. In bivalves it forms the gill chamber and also in those gastropods whose gills, owing to torsion, are above the head. In pulmonates (land snails) it becomes modified into a lung chamber. The mouth and anus are situated within it.
Mantle edge	The margin of the cloak or skirt formed by the mantle. It largely secretes the shell from special glands and is in many cases thickened or reinforced with muscles.
Mid-dorsal line	The hinge line of bivalves. The spiral midway between the sutures in coiled gastropods. The middle line from head to tail in chitons. The line from the upper middle of the margin of the front aperture to that of the rear aperture in tusk shells. The line over the cone in cephalopods from between the eyes on the back of the head to the siphon.
Monomyarian (adj.)	Having only one adductor muscle (the posterior).

Nacre	Pearly deposit lining the inside of the shell.
Nacreous layer	The innermost layer, made of nacre, of the three layers of which the shell is composed.
Operculum	Literally 'little lid'. The horny or calcareous disc or plug which is developed on the back of the foot of many coiled gastropods and serves to close the aperture of the shell.
Outer lip	Outer margin of the aperture of gastropods from the base of the columella to the suture. Sometimes thickened.
Pallial line	The line inside the margin of the valve in bivalves which marks the resting place of the mantle edge in the closed shell during life.
Pallial sinus	The indentation of the pallial line which marks the position of the siphons during life.
Pallium	See mantle.
Parietal area	Thickened part of the inner lip of gastropods.
Perforate (adj.)	Having an umbilicus (q.v.).
Periostracum	The outer, horny, brown layer of the shell which often wears off.
Protoconch (Gastropods) Prodissoconch (Bivalves)	The apical whorls or apical portion of the shell which is formed in the embryonic or larval stage of the animal's life.
Radula	The toothed, rasping, file-like organ protrusible from the mouth of most gastropods, chitons and scaphopoda but not lamellibranchs (bivalves).
Ribs	Or costae. Raised sculpturings running vertically in gastropods, radially in limpets and bivalves.

Ridges   Raised sculpturings running spirally in gastropods, concentrically in limpets and bivalves.

Right valve   Applied to bivalves. The valve on the right of the mid-dorsal line.

Scalariform (adj.)   Ladder-like or stair-like. Whorls not joined but making a loose spiral like a convolvulus stem.

Sculpture, sculpturing   Raised pattern or ornamentation on a shell.

Sinistral   Left-handed shell in coiled gastropods. The spiral winds anti-clockwise from the apex to the aperture which is on the left hand of the spire (see dextral).

Siphon   The tubular extensions of the mantle margin for the inflow (inhalent) or outflow (exhalent) of water to and from the mantle cavity. The tubes may be reinforced with muscles and their two apertures may be either close together or separated. The inhalent siphon is the lower and the exhalent the upper of the two tubes.

Siphonal canal   The extension of the margin of the aperture of a gastropod shell embracing the siphon.

Siphonostomatous (adj.)   Literally 'siphon-mouthed'. The lip of the aperture has a notch or canal for the protrusion of the siphon in gastropods.

Spire   All the whorls of a coiled shell except the last and largest.

Suture/s   The continuous spiral line which marks the junction of the whorls in gastropods, or the lines on the outside of the shell of cephalopods (living

	and fossil) which mark the divisions or septa between the chambers.
Taxodont (adj.)	Term applied to a condition of the teeth of bivalves where there are numerous small teeth along the hinge alternating with sockets.
Teeth	Projections along the hinge of bivalves articulating the two valves.
Umbilicus	The opening at the base of the spiral (not the aperture) in coiled shells. When an umbilicus is present the columella (q.v.) is hollow.
Varix	A specially pronounced rib formed by the mantle edge during a pause in the growth of a gastropod shell.
Ventricose (adj.)	Whorls swollen or bulbous.
Whorl	One complete coil of a spiral shell.

APPENDIX III

SOME RECOMMENDED BOOKS

BARRETT, JOHN, and YONGE, C. M. *Pocket Guide to the Seashore*. Collins, London, reprinted 1965.
Lists the commoner species of British marine molluscs as well as other plants and animals of the sea shore. Well and profusely illustrated in colour and in black and white.

DANCE, PETER S. *Shell Collecting: An Illustrated History*. Faber & Faber, London, 1966.
A history, illustrated by line drawings and colour plates, of the pursuit and art of shell collecting, by a specialist in the Mollusca section of the British Museum (Natural History).

EALES, N. B. *The Littoral Fauna of the British Isles: A Handbook for Collectors*. Cambridge University Press, 1961.
A very useful guide to the sea shore with keys to families. Illustrated in line.

STEP, EDWARD. *Shell Life*. Frederick Warne, London.
One of the famous *Wayside and Woodland* series. Unfortunately out of print at the time of going to press but understood to be reprinting.

STREET, PHILIP. *Shell Life on the Seashore*. Faber & Faber, London, 1961.
Pleasantly written and informative with good line drawings. Not a handbook.

TEBBLE, NORMAN. *British Bivalve Seashells*. British Museum, London, 1966.
A useful guide with keys to lamellibranch species, by a specialist in the Mollusca section of the British Museum (Natural History), South Kensington. Well illustrated in line and colour.

Turk, Stella M. *Collecting Shells*. W. & G. Foyle Ltd., 1966.
A pocket book of information about the hobby of shell collecting: not a handbook. Illustrated with photographs and line drawings.

Yonge, C. M. *The Sea Shore*. Collins, London, reprinted 1961.
A title in the famous *Collins New Naturalist Series*: scholarly and well written by a distinguished marine zoologist and malacologist. Beautifully illustrated by means of coloured and black and white photographs, and line drawings.

INDEX

Abalone, 64, Fig. 16, 135
Abra alba, 89; *A. tenuis*, 89
Acanthocardia echinata, 106
Acanthochitona crinita, Plate 1
Acmaea tessulata, 61, Fig. 16;
   A. virginea, 61
Actaeon tornatilis, 83-4, Fig. 24
Africa, 143-4; East, 140
Akera bullata, 91, Plate 10
America, Central, 139; *see also* United
   States of America
American Indians, 144
Ammonites, 33, 153, 156, 158, 159,
   160, 163; Ceratites, 158
Ammonoids *see* ammonites
Amphineura *see* Coat of Mail shells
Annelida *see* Worms
Anomia epihippum, 67, 95, Fig. 27
Aplysia punctata, 20, 21, 23, Fig. 4, 128
Aporrhais pes-pelecani, 110-11, Fig. 30
Arca tetragona, 67-8, Fig. 18
Architectonia perspectiva, 22, Fig. 3
Architectonidae, 22, Fig. 3
Arcidae, 68
Argonauta, 20, 30, 33-5, Fig. 9
Ark shell, 67-8, Fig. 18
Arthropoda, 18
Artica islandica, Fig. 19, 73
Astarte triangularis, 106, Fig. 29
Atlanta, 129, Fig. 34
Atlantic Ocean, 126-9
Australia, 139
Avicula squamata, 139

Bahamas, 145
Balanus balanoides, Fig. 10, 37, 52
Barleeia, 59
Barnacles, 56-7, 59, 68, Plate 9;
   Acorn, Fig. 10, 37, 52; Stalked,
   Fig. 10, 37
Barnea candida, 117; *B. parva*, 117

Barrett, John and Yonge, C. M.,
   Pocket Guide to the Seashore, 172
Basket shell, 109, Fig. 29
Belemnites, Fig. 36, 158-60, 163
Belemnoids *see* Belemnites
Bittium reticulatum, 58
Bivalves, 20, 26-30, Fig. 7, 35, 47-8,
   111; borers, 113-22; burrowing,
   70-82; Commensalism in, 146-7;
   fossil, 155-6, 158, 163; in mud, 89-
   90; Planktonic, 28-30, 65, 73,
   76-7; on rocks, 64-9; symbiosis in,
   148-51; technical terms applied to,
   164-71
Borers, 113-24, 148; in rock, 113-18,
   148; in wood, 113-24
Botryllus, 59
Brachiopoda, Fig. 11, 38, 160
Breeding habits, 24, 30, 33, 59, 61,
   Plate 6, 65, 93, 119, 122, 124
British rocks, 162-3
Brittle Stars, 147
Brunel, Isambard Kingdom, 120
Brunel, Sir Marc Isambard, 120
Bubble shells, 23, 84, 91, Plate 10
Buccinum undatum, 24, 58, 92-3
Buckie, 24, 58, 92-3
Bullidae, 23 *see also* Sea-slugs
Burrowing shells, 68-9, 70-84; bi-
   valves, 70-82; gastropods, 82-4
Busycon carica, 144; *B. contrarium*, 21

California, Gulf of, 139
Calliostoma zizyphinum, 55, Plate 5
Calyptraea chinensis, Fig. 16, 64, 94
Cambrian rocks, 20, 155, 162
Cameos, 142
Capulus ungaricus, 94-5, Plate 11
Carapus, 135-6
Carboniferous rocks, 156, 162
Cardiidae, 29

175

12